Songs of Ourselves

Volume 3

Cambridge International Education
Anthology of Poetry in English

Shaftesbury Road, Cambridge CB2 8BS, United Kingdom

One Liberty Plaza, 20th Floor, New York, NY 10006, USA

477 Williamstown Road, Port Melbourne, VIC 3207, Australia

314–321, 3rd Floor, Plot 3, Splendor Forum, Jasola District Centre, New Delhi – 110025, India

103 Penang Road, #05–06/07, Visioncrest Commercial, Singapore 238467

Cambridge University Press & Assessment is part of the University of Cambridge.

It furthers the University's mission by disseminating knowledge in the pursuit of education, learning and research at the highest international levels of excellence.

www.cambridge.org

Information on this title: www.cambridge.org/9781009467667 (Paperback)

© Cambridge University Press & Assessment 2025

This publication is in copyright. Subject to statutory exception and to the provisions of relevant collective licensing agreements, no reproduction of any part may take place without the written permission of Cambridge University Press & Assessment.

First published 2025

20 19 18 17 16 15 14 13 12 11 10 9 8 7 6 5 4 3 2 1

Printed in Malaysia by Vivar Printing

A catalogue record for this publication is available from the British Library

ISBN 978-1-009-46766-7 Paperback

ISBN 978-1-009-46764-3 Digital Access (1 Year)

ISBN 978-1-009-46767-4 eBook

Cambridge University Press & Assessment has no responsibility for the persistence or accuracy of URLs for external or third-party internet websites referred to in this publication, and does not guarantee that any content on such websites is, or will remain, accurate or appropriate. Information regarding prices, travel timetables, and other factual information given in this work is correct at the time of first printing but Cambridge University Press & Assessment does not guarantee the accuracy of such information thereafter.

NOTICE TO TEACHERS

It is illegal to reproduce any part of this work in material form (including photocopying and electronic storage) except under the following circumstances:

(i) where you are abiding by a licence granted to your school or institution by the Copyright Licensing Agency;

(ii) where no such licence exists, or where you wish to exceed the terms of a licence, and you have gained the written permission of Cambridge University Press & Assessment;

(iii) where you are allowed to reproduce without permission under the provisions of Chapter 3 of the Copyright, Designs and Patents Act 1988, which covers, for example, the reproduction of short passages within certain types of educational anthology and reproduction for the purposes of setting examination questions.

Every effort has been made to trace the owners of copyright material included in this book. The publishers would be grateful for any omissions to be brought to their notice for acknowledgement in future editions of the book.

Cambridge Dedicated Teacher Awards 2024

Our **Cambridge Dedicated Teacher Awards** are an opportunity to show appreciation for the incredible work teachers do every day.

Thank you to everyone who nominated this year; we have been inspired and moved by all of your stories. Well done to all of our nominees for your dedication to learning and for inspiring the next generation of thinkers, leaders and innovators.

Congratulations to our winners!

Global Winner
South East Asia & Pacific
Sydney Engelbert
Keningau Vocational College, Malaysia

East Asia
Pengfei Jiang
Zhuji Ronghuai Foreign Language School, China

Pakistan
Saeeda Salim
SISA - School of International Studies in Sciences & Arts, Pakistan

South Asia
Meena Mishra
Dr Sarvepalli Radhakrishnan International School, India

Middle East and North Africa
Gina Justus
Our Own English High school- Sharjah- Girls, United Arab Emirates

Sub-Saharan Africa
Tajudeen Odufeso
Isara Secondary School, Isara Remo, Nigeria

Europe
Aynur Bayazit
Menekşe Ahmet Yalçınkaya Kindergarten, Türkiye

Latin America & the Caribbean
Ramon Majé Floriano
Montessori sede San Francisco, Colombia

North America
Marisa Santos
Seminole Ridge Community High School, United States

For more information about our dedicated teachers and their stories, go to dedicatedteacher.cambridge.org

Contents

Introduction ... 4

PART 1
Natural Encounters

1. *Sonnet 129* ... 2
   PETRARCH

2. *The Bird* ... 3
   HENRY VAUGHAN

3. *Of Many Worlds in This World* ... 5
   MARGARET CAVENDISH

4. from *The Offering* ... 6
   LADY MARY CHUDLEIGH

5. *To the Nightingale* ... 8
   ANNE FINCH

6. *To the Insect of the Gossamer* ... 10
   CHARLOTTE SMITH

7. *Ode to a Nightingale* ... 11
   JOHN KEATS

8. *The Caterpillar* ... 15
   ANNA LAETITIA BARBAULD

9. *Insects* ... 17
   JOHN CLARE

10. *Binsey Poplars* ... 19
    GERARD MANLEY HOPKINS

11. *A Bird came down the Walk* ... 21
    EMILY DICKINSON

Contents

12	*The Panther* RAINER MARIA RILKE	23
13	*Autumn* MELISSÁNTHI	24
14	*The Other Tiger* JORGE LUIS BORGES	26
15	*A Blessing* JAMES WRIGHT	28
16	*Penguin on the Beach* RUTH MILLER	30
17	*Oblivion* ELLIS AYITEY KOMEY	32
18	*Suns and Straws* DOROTHY DONNELLY	34
19	*Water of Jellyfish* CORAL BRACHO	36
20	*Toroa: Albatross* HONE TUWHARE	39
21	*On the Random Distribution of King Parrots* JOHN KINSELLA	40
22	*The Camel Comes to Us from the Barbarians* RITA DOVE	42
23	*Frog* MARILÈNE PHIPPS	44
24	from *Endless Inter-States* SINA QUEYRAS	46
25	*The Whale* KATRINA PORTEOUS	48
26	*Fox* ALICE OSWALD	50

27	*#ExtinctionRebellion* PASCALE PETIT	52
28	*The Sun Wanders, Searching for Shade* ALARI	54
29	*Whale* CINDY BOTHA	56
30	*The Year of One Thousand Fires* ANDRÉ NAFFIS-SAHELY	58

PART 2
People and Places

31	*The Garden* ANDREW MARVELL	62
32	from *Trivia* JOHN GAY	65
33	from *The Deserted Village* OLIVER GOLDSMITH	67
34	from *In Memoriam* ALFRED, LORD TENNYSON	69
35	*I Saw Red Evening Through the Rain* ROBERT LOUIS STEVENSON	70
36	from *Our Casuarina Tree* TORU DUTT	72
37	*Fair Weather* DOROTHY PARKER	73
38	*Glory* MARY URSULA BETHELL	74
39	*Deep in the Hills* RUTH DALLAS	75
40	*Angola* AMÉLIA VEIGA	76

Contents

41	*O Earth* SIRIMAN CISSOKO	78
42	*The Sash Window* ROSEMARY TONKS	80
43	*The Echoes* MAZISI KUNENE	82
44	*Londoners* KRISTINA RUNGANO	84
45	*An Old Colonial Building* LEUNG PING-KWAN	86
46	*Perhaps the World Ends Here* JOY HARJO	88
47	*My Aunts Don't Want to Move* MONIZA ALVI	90
48	*Map Store* IMAN MERSAL	91
49	*Under These Stones* DELORES GAUNTLETT	93
50	*Nomad in the Sunset* ROZA MUKASHEVA	95
51	*Leaving Fingerprints* IMTIAZ DHARKER	97
52	*Ruin* JACOB POLLEY	99
53	*Till* GREGOR ADDISON	101
54	*I Pick Up My Footprints* VASYL HOLOBORODKO	102
55	*Sentinel* JENNIFER ANNE CHAMPION	104

56	*Grandmothers Abroad* TISHANI DOSHI	106
57	*Paradise* ROGER ROBINSON	108
58	*House* HANNAH LOWE	109
59	*Knots* JO CLEMENT	110
60	*Touchstone* OLIVE SENIOR	111

PART 3
Play

61	*Gratiana Dancing and Singing* RICHARD LOVELACE	114
62	from *Ode for Musicke on St Cecilia's Day* ALEXANDER POPE	116
63	from *The Art of Dancing* SOAME JENYNS	118
64	from *The Paper Kite* SAMUEL BOWDEN	120
65	from *Cricket. An Heroic Poem* JAMES DANCE	122
66	from *The Prelude* WILLIAM WORDSWORTH	125
67	from *Andromeda* CHARLES KINGSLEY	126
68	from *A Swimmer's Dream* ALGERNON CHARLES SWINBURNE	128
69	*The Blind Musician* JAMES T FRANKLIN	130

Contents

70	*Untitled* OSIP MANDELSTAM	133
71	*when faces called flowers float out of the ground* E E CUMMINGS	135
72	*Song* SEÁN Ó RÍORDÁIN	136
73	*In Georgia* YEVGENY YEVTUSHENKO	138
74	*The Day Lady Died* FRANK O'HARA	140
75	*Allegro* TOMAS TRANSTRÖMER	142
76	*The Joy of Writing* WISŁAWA SZYMBORSKA	143
77	*Untitled* MARIO LUZI	145
78	*Swimming after Thoughts* JAY PARINI	147
79	*Bouncing Boy* HELEN DUNMORE	149
80	*Captain of the Lighthouse* TOGARA MUZANENHAMO	151
81	*Lightness* YVONNE GRAY	152
82	*Pier* VONA GROARKE	154
83	*Common\wealth* NII AYIKWEI PARKES	155
84	*Prologue (Grime Mix)* PATIENCE AGBABI	157

85	*Handfast* VAHNI CAPILDEO	159
86	*Girl in the Blue Pool* HELEN DUNMORE	161
87	*The Kite* ANDREW WYNN OWEN	163
88	*Huia* BILL MANHIRE	165
89	*Sea: Night Surfing in Bolinas* FORREST GANDER	167
90	*How to Perfect a Flip Turn* CYNTHIA MILLER	169

PART 4
Relationships

91	*Sonnet 106* WILLIAM SHAKESPEARE	172
92	*On My First Son* BEN JONSON	173
93	*The Bait* JOHN DONNE	174
94	*To His Coy Mistress* ANDREW MARVELL	176
95	*To the Ladies* LADY MARY CHUDLEIGH	178
96	*First Love* JOHN CLARE	180
97	*I Wish I Could Remember That First Day* CHRISTINA ROSSETTI	182
98	*Never the Time and the Place* ROBERT BROWNING	183

Contents

99	*The Sorrow of Love* WILLIAM BUTLER YEATS	184
100	*My Heart Shall Be Thy Garden* ALICE MEYNELL	185
101	*The Gardener (3)* RABINDRANATH TAGORE	186
102	*Lover's Return* LANGSTON HUGHES	187
103	*The Poet Speaks to His Love on the Telephone* FEDERICO GARCÍA LORCA	189
104	*Sea Canes* DEREK WALCOTT	190
105	*'The Poppy Signals Time to Scythe the Wheat'* MIMI KHALVATI	192
106	*Temporary Sanity* DAMBUDZO MARECHERA	193
107	*Transit* MICHEAL O'SIADHAIL	194
108	*Words Between Us* DEBJANI CHATTERJEE	195
109	*Song* JENNIFER RAHIM	197
110	*The Sculpture* AMINUR RAHMAN	199
111	*A Feather* SHAKILA AZIZZADA	200
112	*Poet, Lover, Birdwatcher* NISSIM EZEKIEL	201
113	*Arguments Left* TOGARA MUZANENHAMO	202

114 *In the Chill* SOPHIE HANNAH	203
115 *Gloves* JOANNA PRESTON	204
116 *Fast Forward* FLEUR ADCOCK	205
117 *You May Have Heard of Me* SHAZEA QURAISHI	206
118 *Netezon Laundrette* CHARLOTTE VAN DEN BROECK	208
119 *Beloved* ASHA LUL MOHAMUD YUSUF	210
120 *Ode to a Pot Noodle* ROMALYN ANTE	213

PART 5
Self

121 *I Am As I Am* THOMAS WYATT	216
122 *My Mind to Me a Kingdom Is* EDWARD DYER	218
123 *Now Leave and Let Me Rest* QUEEN ELIZABETH I	221
124 *Sonnet 91* WILLIAM SHAKESPEARE	223
125 *Sonnet 7* JOHN MILTON	224
126 from *Essay on Happiness* MARY LEAPOR	225
127 from *The Happy Solitude* ANNA WILLIAMS	227

Contents

128 *On Virtue* PHILLIS WHEATLEY	230
129 *Dedication* (from *Faust*) JOHANN WOLFGANG VON GOETHE	231
130 from *Lara, a Tale* GEORGE GORDON, LORD BYRON	233
131 *Thoughts on My Sick-Bed* DOROTHY WORDSWORTH	235
132 *Long Time a Child* HARTLEY COLERIDGE	238
133 *Stanzas: 'Often rebuked, yet always back returning'* EMILY BRONTË	239
134 from *My Heart and I* ELIZABETH BARRETT BROWNING	241
135 *What the Heart Is Like* MIROSLAV HOLUB	243
136 *The Widower in the Country* LES MURRAY	245
137 from *Solitude* TOMAS TRANSTRÖMER	247
138 Two short poems from *Letters to Martha* DENNIS BRUTUS	249
139 *Epitaph* TCHICAYA U TAM'SI	250
140 *You Won't Believe It* SIMIN BEHBAHANI	251
141 *Mistress of My Own Being* IFI AMADIUME	253
142 *What I Learned in the Wars* YEHUDA AMICHAI	255

143 *Narcissus at the Flea Market* JOHN AGARD	257
144 *Bones* ARUNDHATHI SUBRAMANIAM	259
145 *The Way I Am* GEORGE THE POET	262
146 *Kindness* NAOMI SHIHAB NYE	263
147 *Kumukanda* KAYO CHINGONYI	265
148 *Maracas Beach Prayer* ROGER ROBINSON	266
149 *The Day* MUKAHANG LIMBU	267
150 *Picture of Girl and Small Boy (Burij, Gaza, 2014)* MARJORIE LOTFI	269
Index of First Lines	270
Acknowledgements	275

Introduction

The borders of human geography are broken only when poetry speaks, and poetry speaks not only about landscapes, but about peoplescapes …

In poetry I am part of other voices in other hearts, but I am also part of the voices of the insects, the birds, the sky, the soil and the air we breathe …

Chenjerai Hove (introduction to *Blind Moon*)

This third volume of *Songs of Ourselves* joins its two predecessors as a collection of poems from around the world, selections from which are set for study for Cambridge International syllabuses at IGCSE, AS and A Level.

However, it is also meant to be enjoyed in itself as an anthology set around interesting and perennial themes, and exhibiting a wide range of styles, forms and ideas. The selection of poems again ranges across the history of poetry – the earliest having been written in the fourteenth century – but there is a renewed emphasis here on modern voices, including many from the twenty-first century.

Poems are chosen to be accessible to students at the relevant levels of study, with subject matter that appeals, while the language, style and form – the *poetry* – both challenges and pleases the reader.

In keeping with previous volumes of *Songs*, this is primarily an anthology of poetry written in English; for this third volume, however, we have also included a number of poems in translation, principally for study for the IGCSE World Literature syllabus. Though these poems will not be set for the Literature in English syllabuses, they may be read in conjunction and follow the same themes.

The poems are presented in five thematic sections, and the themes are broad and flexible. Within these sections, poems are in chronological order, by date of first publication. (Occasionally, this date may be significantly later than when the poem was written, in which case this is noted.)

But poems are as slippery as eels when it comes to being classified – they don't always like it. We need to beware of thinking a poem can be easily or simply pinned down, and instead choose to read it carefully – out loud as well as silently – to get to know it well, thinking about the form, the shape, the structure, the imagery, the voice or voices within it and its use of rhythm and rhyme. Comparing two poems is often a good way of getting to know each of them individually in more depth, and there are many opportunities within this volume for putting two poems together which share a theme, an idea or a mood.

Introduction

Volume 3 is both a stand-alone book and a companion to Volumes 1 and 2. As well as continuing the thread of poems by well-known poets from the established academic canon of English literature, it introduces many new and perhaps some unfamiliar names. Indeed, in recognition and celebration of the diversity of the Cambridge learner community, the poets chosen for inclusion here represent a total of over fifty countries, each bringing a unique set of values, experiences and perspectives to their work. It is interesting to observe both the distinctive styles and preoccupations in different cultures, as well as the similarities, as they often focus on universal human concerns, and they also often refer to some shared literary heritage.

As Chenjerai Hove says in the quotation above, poetry is a way to cross boundaries and also gives a voice to the creatures and landscapes of our Earth, at a time when we need to listen to its voice more urgently than ever before.

Each poem does stand on its own merits, but it can be very rewarding to seek out further poems by the poets in this book – using libraries or the internet – and it can be great fun to do so, making all sorts of new discoveries. We live in a golden age for poetry, with many young poets using English to speak to a bigger audience than ever.

I hope you enjoy the book and make some new discoveries of your own.

Editor's acknowledgements

With grateful thanks to the staff at the Cambridge Central Public Library, University Library, the Cambridge English Faculty Library and the Cambridge African Studies library, with appreciation for the work our librarians do.

Note on selections

The poems in this collection were chosen primarily by Mary Wilmer alongside Tim Underhill and Peter Johnston, with additional recommendations both from colleagues at Cambridge International (including Sonia Attwell, David Blaikie, Tricia Harriss and Kevin O'Grady) and from a range of contributors from our wider global Cambridge community.

PART 1

Natural Encounters

1

Sonnet 129

O joyous, blossoming, ever-blessed flowers!
'Mid which my queen her gracious footstep sets;
O plain, that keep'st her words for amulets
And hold'st her memory in thy leafy bowers!
　O trees, with earliest green of spring-time hours,
And spring-time's pale and tender violets!
O grove so dark, the proud sun only lets
His blithe rays gild the outskirts of your towers!
　O pleasant country-side! O purest stream,
That mirrorest her sweet face, her eyes so clear,
And of their living light can catch the beam!
　I envy you her haunts so close and dear.
There is no rock so senseless but I deem
It burns with passion that to mine is near.

Petrarch (14th century); T W Higginson (translated 1867)

2

The Bird

Hither thou com'st: the busy wind all night
Blew through thy lodging, where thy own warm wing
Thy pillow was. Many a sullen storm
(For which course man seems much the fitter born)
    Rained on thy bed
    And harmless head.

And now as fresh and cheerful as the light
Thy little heart in early hymns doth sing
Unto that *Providence*, whose unseen arm
Curbed them, and clothed thee well and warm.
    All things that be, praise him; and had
    Their lesson taught them, when first made.

So hills and valleys into singing break,
And though poor stones have neither speech nor tongue,
While active winds and streams both run and speak,
Yet stones are deep in admiration.
Thus praise and prayer here beneath the sun
Make lesser mornings, when the great are done.

The Bird

    For each inclosèd spirit is a star
        Enlightening his own little sphere,
Whose light, though fetched and borrowèd from far,
        Both mornings makes, and evenings there.

But as these birds of light make a land glad,
Chirping their solemn Matins on each tree:
So in the shades of night some dark fowls be,
Whose heavy notes make all that hear them, sad.

    The turtle then in palm-trees mourns,
        While owls and satyrs howl;
    The pleasant land to brimstone turns
        And all her streams grow foul.

Brightness and mirth, and love and faith, all fly,
Till the Day-spring breaks forth again from high.

                Henry Vaughan (1655)

Of Many Worlds in This World

Just like as in a nest of boxes round,
Degrees of sizes in each box are found:
So, in this world, may many others be
Thinner and less, and less still by degree:
Although they are not subject to our sense,
A world may be no bigger than two-pence.
Nature is curious, and such works may shape,
Which our dull senses easily escape:
For creatures, small as atoms, may be there,
If every one a creature's figure bear.
If atoms four, a world can make, then see
What several worlds might in an ear-ring be:
For, millions of those atoms may be in
The head of one small, little, single pin.
And if thus small, then ladies may well wear
A world of worlds, as pendents in each ear.

Margaret Cavendish (1668)

from *The Offering*

1

Accept, my God, the Praises which I bring,
The humble Tribute from a Creature due:
   Permit me of thy Pow'r to sing,
That Pow'r which did stupendous Wonders do,
And whose Effects we still with awful Rev'rence view:
That mighty Pow'r which from thy boundless Store,
   Out of thy self where all things lay,
   This beauteous Universe did call,
This Great, this Glorious, this amazing All!
And fill'd with Matter that vast empty Space,
   Where nothing all alone
Had long unrival'd sat on its triumphant Throne.
   See! now in every place
   The restless Atoms play:
   Lo! High as Heav'n they proudly soar,
   And fill the wide-stretch'd Regions there;
In Suns they shine Above, in Gems Below,
And roll in solid Masses thro' the yielding Air:
In Earth compacted, and diffus'd in Seas;
In Corn they nourish, and in Flow'rs they please:
   In Beasts they walk, in Birds they fly,

And in gay painted Insects croud the Skie:

In Fish amid the Silver Waves they stray,

And ev'ry where the Laws of their first Cause obey:

    Of them, compos'd with wondrous Art,

        We are our selves a part:

And on us still they Nutriment bestow;

To us they kindly come, from us they swiftly go,

And thro' our Veins in Purple Torrents flow.

    Vacuity is no where found,

Each Place is full: with bodies we're encompass'd round:

    In Sounds they're to our Ears convey'd,

In fragrant Odors they our Smell delight,

And in Ten thousand curious Forms display'd,

        They entertain our Sight:

    In luscious Fruits our Tast they court,

And in cool balmy Breezes round us sport,

The friendly Zephyrs fan our vital Flame,

And give us Breath to praise his holy Name,

From whom our selves, and all these Blessings came.

                Lady Mary Chudleigh (1710)

5

To the Nightingale

Exert thy Voice, sweet Harbinger of Spring!
    This Moment is thy Time to sing,
    This Moment I attend to Praise,
And set my Numbers to thy Layes.
    Free as thine shall be my Song;
    As thy Musick, short, or long.
Poets, wild as thee, were born,
    Pleasing best when unconfin'd,
    When to Please is least design'd,
Soothing but their Cares to rest;
    Cares do still their Thoughts molest,
    And still th' unhappy Poet's Breast,
Like thine, when best he sings, is plac'd against a Thorn.
She begins, Let all be still!
    Muse, thy Promise now fulfill!
Sweet, oh! sweet, still sweeter yet
Can thy Words such Accents fit,
Canst thou Syllables refine,
Melt a Sense that shall retain
Still some Spirit of the Brain,
Till with Sounds like these it join.

  'Twill not be! then change thy Note;
  Let division shake thy Throat.
Hark! Division now she tries;
Yet as far the Muse outflies.
  Cease then, prithee, cease thy Tune;
  Trifler, wilt thou sing till *June?*
Till thy Bus'ness all lies waste,
And the Time of Building's past!
  Thus we Poets that have Speech,
Unlike what thy Forests teach,
  If a fluent Vein be shown
  That's transcendent to our own,
  Criticize, reform, or preach,
  Or censure what we cannot reach.

           Anne Finch (1713)

6

To the Insect of the Gossamer

Small, viewless Æronaut, that by the line
    Of Gossamer suspended, in mid air
    Float'st on a sun beam – Living Atom, where
Ends thy breeze-guided voyage; – with what design
In Æther dost thou launch thy form minute,
    Mocking the eye? – Alas! before the veil
Of denser clouds shall hide thee, the pursuit
    Of the keen Swift may end thy fairy sail! –
Thus on the golden thread that Fancy weaves
    Buoyant, as Hope's illusive flattery breathes,
The young and visionary Poet leaves
    Life's dull realities, while sevenfold wreaths
Of rainbow light around his head revolve.
Ah! soon at Sorrow's touch the radiant dreams dissolve!

                                               Charlotte Smith (1797)

7

Ode to a Nightingale

I

My heart aches, and a drowsy numbness pains
  My sense, as though of hemlock I had drunk,
Or emptied some dull opiate to the drains
  One minute past, and Lethe-wards had sunk:
'Tis not through envy of thy happy lot,
  But being too happy in thine happiness –
    That thou, light-wingèd Dryad of the trees,
      In some melodious plot
  Of beechen green, and shadows numberless,
    Singest of summer in full-throated ease.

II

O, for a draught of vintage! that hath been
  Cooled a long age in the deep-delvèd earth,
Tasting of Flora and the country green,
  Dance, and Provençal song, and sunburnt mirth!
O for a beaker full of the warm South,
  Full of the true, the blushful Hippocrene,
    With beaded bubbles winking at the brim,
      And purple-stainèd mouth,

That I might drink, and leave the world unseen,
  And with thee fade away into the forest dim –

III

Fade far away, dissolve, and quite forget
  What thou among the leaves hast never known,
The weariness, the fever, and the fret
  Here, where men sit and hear each other groan;
Where palsy shakes a few, sad, last grey hairs,
  Where youth grows pale, and spectre-thin, and dies;
    Where but to think is to be full of sorrow
      And leaden-eyed despairs;
Where Beauty cannot keep her lustrous eyes,
  Or new Love pine at them beyond to-morrow.

IV

Away! away! for I will fly to thee,
  Not charioted by Bacchus and his pards,
But on the viewless wings of Poesy,
  Though the dull brain perplexes and retards.
Already with thee! tender is the night,
  And haply the Queen-Moon is on her throne,
    Clustered around by all her starry Fays;
      But here there is no light,
Save what from heaven is with the breezes blown
    Through verdurous glooms and winding mossy ways.

V

I cannot see what flowers are at my feet,
  Nor what soft incense hangs upon the boughs,
But, in embalmèd darkness, guess each sweet
  Wherewith the seasonable month endows
The grass, the thicket, and the fruit-tree wild –
  White hawthorn, and the pastoral eglantine;
    Fast fading violets covered up in leaves;
      And mid-May's eldest child,
  The coming musk-rose, full of dewy wine,
    The murmurous haunt of flies on summer eves.

VI

Darkling I listen; and, for many a time
  I have been half in love with easeful Death,
Called him soft names in many a musèd rhyme,
  To take into the air my quiet breath;
Now more than ever seems it rich to die,
  To cease upon the midnight with no pain,
    While thou art pouring forth thy soul abroad
      In such an ecstasy!
  Still wouldst thou sing, and I have ears in vain –
    To thy high requiem become a sod.

VII

Thou wast not born for death, immortal Bird!
  No hungry generations tread thee down;
The voice I hear this passing night was heard
  In ancient days by emperor and clown:
Perhaps the self-same song that found a path

7 Ode to a Nightingale

    Through the sad heart of Ruth, when, sick for home,
      She stood in tears amid the alien corn;
        The same that oft-times hath
    Charmed magic casements, opening on the foam
      Of perilous seas, in faery lands forlorn.

VIII

Forlorn! the very word is like a bell
  To toll me back from thee to my sole self!
Adieu! the fancy cannot cheat so well
  As she is famed to do, deceiving elf.
Adieu! adieu! thy plaintive anthem fades
  Past the near meadows, over the still stream,
    Up the hill-side; and now 'tis buried deep
      In the next valley-glades:
Was it a vision, or a waking dream?
  Fled is that music – Do I wake or sleep?

John Keats (1819)

8

The Caterpillar

No, helpless thing, I cannot harm thee now;
Depart in peace, thy little life is safe,
For I have scanned thy form with curious eye,
Noted the silver line that streaks thy back,
The azure and the orange that divide
Thy velvet sides; thee, houseless wanderer,
My garment has enfolded, and my arm
Felt the light pressure of thy hairy feet;
Thou hast curled round my finger; from its tip,
Precipitous descent! with stretched out neck,
Bending thy head in airy vacancy,
This way and that, inquiring, thou hast seemed
To ask protection; now, I cannot kill thee.
Yet I have sworn perdition to thy race,
And recent from the slaughter am I come
Of tribes and embryo nations: I have sought
With sharpened eye and persecuting zeal,
Where, folded in their silken webs they lay
Thriving and happy; swept them from the tree
And crushed whole families beneath my foot;
Or, sudden, poured on their devoted heads
The vials of destruction. – This I've done,

8   The Caterpillar

Nor felt the touch of pity: but when thou, –
A single wretch, escaped the general doom,
Making me feel and clearly recognise
Thine individual existence, life,
And fellowship of sense with all that breathes, –
Present'st thyself before me, I relent,
And cannot hurt thy weakness. – So the storm
Of horrid war, o'erwhelming cities, fields,
And peaceful villages, rolls dreadful on:
The victor shouts triumphant; he enjoys
The roar of cannon and the clang of arms,
And urges, by no soft relentings stopped,
The work of death and carnage. Yet should one,
A single sufferer from the field escaped,
Panting and pale, and bleeding at his feet,
Lift his imploring eyes, – the hero weeps;
He is grown human, and capricious Pity,
Which would not stir for thousands, melts for one
With sympathy spontaneous: – 'Tis not Virtue,
Yet 'tis the weakness of a virtuous mind.

Anna Laetitia Barbauld (1825)

9

Insects

Thou tiney loiterer on the barleys beard
& happy unit of a numerous herd
Of playfellows the laughing summer brings
Mocking the sunshine in their glittering wings
How merrily they creep & run & flye
No kin they bear to labours drudgery
Smoothing the velvet of the pale hedge rose
& where they flye for dinner no one knows
The dewdrops feed them not – they love the shine
Of noon whose sun may bring them golden wine
All day theyre playing in their sunday dress
Till night goes sleep & they can do no less
Then in the heath bells silken hood they flie
& like to princes in their slumber lie
From coming night & dropping dews & all
In silken beds & roomy painted hall
So happily they spend their summer day
Now in the cornfields now the new mown hay
One almost fancys that such happy things
In coloured hoods & richly burnished wings

9   Insects

>Are fairy folk in splendid masquerade
>Disguised through fear of mortal folk affraid
>Keeping their merry pranks a mystery still
>Lest glaring day should do their secrets ill

John Clare (1835)

10

Binsey Poplars

Felled 1879

My aspens dear, whose airy cages quelled,
Quelled or quenched in leaves the leaping sun,
All felled, felled, are all felled;
   Of a fresh and following folded rank
      Not spared, not one
      That dandled a sandalled
    Shadow that swam or sank
On meadow and river and wind-wandering weed-winding bank.

O if we but knew what we do
      When we delve or hew –
Hack and rack the growing green!
      Since country is so tender
To touch, her being só slender,
That, like this sleek and seeing ball
But a prick will make no eye at all,
Where we, even where we mean
      To mend her we end her,

10   Binsey Poplars

        When we hew or delve:
After-comers cannot guess the beauty been.
  Ten or twelve, only ten or twelve
    Strokes of havoc únselve
        The sweet especial scene,
  Rural scene, a rural scene,
  Sweet especial rural scene.

Gerard Manley Hopkins (1879)

# 11

A Bird came down the Walk

A Bird came down the Walk –
He did not know I saw –
He bit an Angleworm in halves
And ate the fellow, raw,

And then he drank a Dew
From a convenient Grass –
And then hopped sidewise to the Wall
To let a Beetle pass –

He glanced with rapid eyes
That hurried all around –
They looked like frightened Beads, I thought –
He stirred his Velvet Head

Like one in danger, Cautious,
I offered him a Crumb
And he unrolled his feathers
And rowed him softer home –

11   A Bird came down the Walk

>Than Oars divide the Ocean,
>Too silver for a seam –
>Or Butterflies, off Banks of Noon
>Leap, plashless as they swim.

Emily Dickinson (1891)

12

The Panther

Jardin des Plantes, Paris

Scanning the bars, his gaze is grown so numb
that there is nothing left that it can hold.
Behind the thousand bars these bars become
to him, it seems as if there is no world.

The padding pace that threatens lope or canter,
turning in circles ever-smaller-sized,
is like a dance of strength around some center
in which a great will stands still, paralyzed.

Only, the pupils' curtain lifts sometimes,
in silence, and an image rushes past,
then down the tensing stillness of the limbs,
and dies deep in the heart made fast.

                              Rainer Maria Rilke (1907); Len Krisak (translated 2015)

13

Autumn

Hour of dusk;

the skirt of the sky is wrung

and hung out to dry by autumn clouds;

and in the recess after rain

the snails come to stroll

under the fading parasol

of the sun ... Now earth,

that lamia, suns her wet wool blankets

adorned with the embellishments of meadows;

and from the grasses

and from the high pastures

waterdrops glide – beads

and pearls

of heavenly rings

that are gathered by Nereids, who weave

in their underground sunless grottoes and seraglios;

candelabra and silvery night lamps

are hung in hollows

and in nets of crystal spheres

by that old sorceress, the spider;

and one by one

insects of every kind

come crawling out of the earth
and from beneath the bark of trees
in a drunken carousal.
An ant clambers onto a blossoming thorn
and gazes at all the world from such a sunny lookout –
there, a furrow of water! –
and loiters lazily.
Over the straw raft, wherever it moors,
the frogs play leapfrog.
An entire cosmos of minute animals
sails in canoes of husks and walnut shells.
A cold shivering falls on the waters,
and now the siphon will strip
the dry leaves from the trees
like a swarm of butterflies.
The wind-shepherd blows his pipe
amid the reeds, and as he goes, goes, goes,
he shoos his flock of summers
to other haunts
and other winter pastures.

Melissánthi (1930); Kimon Friar (translated 1973)

The Other Tiger

> And the craft createth a semblance.
> Morris, *Sigurd the Volsung* (1876)

I think of a tiger. The fading light enhances
the vast complexities of the Library
and seems to set the bookshelves at a distance;
powerful, innocent, bloodstained, and new-made,
it will prowl through its jungle and its morning
and leave its footprint on the muddy edge
of a river with a name unknown to it
(in its world, there are no names, nor past, nor future,
only the sureness of the present moment)
and it will cross the wilderness of distance
and sniff out in the woven labyrinth
of smells the smell peculiar to morning
and the scent on the air of deer, delectable.
Behind the lattice of bamboo, I notice
its stripes, and I sense its skeleton
under the magnificence of the quivering skin.
In vain the convex oceans and the deserts
spread themselves across the earth between us;
from this one house in a far-off seaport
in South America, I dream you, follow you,
oh tiger on the fringes of the Ganges.

The Other Tiger

Evening spreads in my spirit and I keep thinking
that the tiger I am calling up in my poem
is a tiger made of symbols and of shadows,
a set of literary images,
scraps remembered from encyclopedias,
and not the deadly tiger, the fateful jewel
that in the sun or the deceptive moonlight
follows its paths, in Bengal or Sumatra,
of love, of indolence, of dying.
Against the tiger of symbols I have set
the real one, the hot-blooded one
that savages a herd of buffalo,
and today, the third of August, '59,
its patient shadow moves across the plain,
but yet, the act of naming it, of guessing
what is its nature and its circumstance
creates a fiction, not a living creature,
not one of those that prowl on the earth.

Let us look for a third tiger. This one
will be a form in my dream like all the others,
a system, an arrangement of human language,
and not the flesh-and-bone tiger
that, out of reach of all mythologies,
paces the earth. I know all this; yet something
drives me to this ancient, perverse adventure,
foolish and vague, yet still I keep on looking
throughout the evening for the other tiger,
the other tiger, the one not in this poem.

                Jorge Luis Borges (1960); Alastair Reid (translated 1972)

15

A Blessing

Just off the highway to Rochester, Minnesota,
Twilight bounds softly forth on the grass.
And the eyes of those two Indian ponies
Darken with kindness.
They have come gladly out of the willows
To welcome my friend and me.
We step over the barbed wire into the pasture
Where they have been grazing all day, alone.
They ripple tensely, they can hardly contain their happiness
That we have come.
They bow shyly as wet swans. They love each other.
There is no loneliness like theirs.
At home once more,
They begin munching the young tufts of spring in the darkness.
I would like to hold the slenderer one in my arms,
For she has walked over to me
And nuzzled my left hand.
She is black and white,
Her mane falls wild on her forehead,
And the light breeze moves me to caress her long ear

That is delicate as the skin over a girl's wrist.
Suddenly I realize
That if I stepped out of my body I would break
Into blossom.

James Wright (1961)

16

Penguin on the Beach

Stranger in his own element,
Sea-casualty, the castaway manikin
Waddles in his tailored coat-tails. Oil

Has spread a deep commercial stain
Over his downy shirtfront. Sleazy, grey,
It clogs the sleekness. Far too well

He must recall the past, to be so cautious:
Watch him step into the waves. He shudders
Under the froth, slides, slips, on the wet sand,

Escaping to dryness, dearth, in a white cascade,
An involuntary shouldering off of gleam.
Hands push him back into the sea. He stands

In pained and silent expostulation.
Once he knew a sunlit, leaping smoothness,
But close within his head's small knoll, and dark

He retains the image: oil on sea,
Green slicks, black lassos of sludge
Sleaving the breakers in a stain-spread scarf.

He shudders now from the clean flinching wave,
Turns and plods back up the yellow sand,
Ineffably weary, triumphantly sad.

He is immensely wise: he trusts nobody. His senses
Are clogged with experience. He eats
Fish from his Saviour's hands, and it tastes black.

Ruth Miller (1965)

Oblivion

I want to remember the fallen palm
With whitening fluid of wine
Dripping from its hardened belly
In this forest of life.

I want to remember it from the road
With mud on my feet,
And thorn-scraped flesh
From the branches by the water.

I want to remember them well
The sight of the green-eyed forest
The jubilant voices of the frogs
And the pleading cries of the owls.

I want to walk among the palms
With their razor-edged leaves
Shadowing the yam and cassava shrubs
Under which the crab builds its castle
And the cocoa pods drooping like mothers
Breasts feeding a hungry child.

I want to remember them all
Before they die and turn to mud
When I have gone.

Ellis Ayitey Komey (1971)

18

Suns and Straws

Though the fall of an apple is not, like the fall
of a star, a spectacular act, *one* apple
rose, as it fell, to comet-fame
when Newton, noting it, saw in the flash
of its fall, the clue to the law of the fall

of all – straws and stones; oak trees
and sparrows and hairs. But earth, like a jealous
shepherd zealous for the sheep of his flock,
draws with her magni-magnet all matter's
scattered fragments back into her keep.

(Mysterious matter – mute, inscrutable,
dark, indestructible stuff! Ever
at the beck of form, it will furnish flesh
for a flea or a flower; or fatten a worm;
or fur a tiger.) Not an atom is lost

from the plump planet's curvaceous figure.
Apple and apple-shaped earth, each
in its orbit, stand or fall by the laws
they're attuned to – the Pied Piper music that all
the spheres hear, that moves the millions of suns

through space and assembles the nebulas' clusters.
What Juggler, balancing galaxies like plates,
set those celestial corollas to spinning,
creating thereby a Versailles of lily-
bright lights and fountains across the sky!

Dorothy Donnelly (1978)

19

Water of Jellyfish

Water of jellyfish,
milky, snaking water
of ever-changing shapes; glossy water-flesh; melting
into its lovely surroundings. Water – sumptuous waters
receding, languid

and layered into calm. Water,
water silken, dusky, dense as lead – mercurial;
       floating free, idling. The seaweed in there,
sparkling, in pleasure's very breast. The
seaweed, crests a-bubbling;

– above the over-arching silence, above the long spits
of basalt rock; the water-weed, its familiar caresses,
its gentle flux. Water of light, of fish; the breeze, the
       agate
spilling its light. The shy elk flicker like flame –

through the cotton-silk trees, through the shoals
of little fish a flame is pulsing,
water slinking, lynx-like; water of bream (jasper's
       sudden reds and browns). Such glory here,

among the jellyfish medusas.
– Parted lips of coastline, the breeze's gentle
      movements,
lulling softly, settling into crystals, amphibious,
lubricious – water, silken and
magnetic; poised. Water, coasting – lascivious radiance

wading, oily,
over crumbling basalt. Light crawls, opal,
through its own inner flames. – Water
of jellyfish.
Sweet fresh-water shine;
water leaving no traces; dense,
mercurial
      white as steel, parting round the granite stacks,
its flashes of minnows; secretive, smooth. – Water alive,

and rolling; a bronze sun vaulting in close;
– liquid minerals, spurting. Water of jellyfish, a water to
      feel
dissolving into itself
into a slick of indigo, quivering honeycombs. Long
      strands of water, sea-lettuce, the catfish nibbling
in its rich, streaming bed, whose light nectars
form a golden pond, liminal. Weightless water,
air inside amber,
– a chrism of light, full of grace; the high tide a tiger,
below a wash of shadow. Water at the edge, water-eel,
swallowing itself,

19   Water of Jellyfish

its great journey by night –
along these matrices of silk, through the
sea-sage. – Water

rich with cod. Heavy water (that calm pleasure,
warm; the way it shimmers) –
Water's edge –

its smooth changes, its delight in itself,
its own seductive rise and fall. Water,
silken, receding, layered
into languid calm. Water, water; its gentle stroke
– water of the otter, the fish. Water

of jellyfish,
milky, snaking; water,

Coral Bracho (1981); Katherine Pierpoint and Tom Boll (translated 2010)

20

Toroa: Albatross

Day and night endlessly you have flown effortless of wing
    over chest-expanding oceans far from land.
    Do you switch on an automatic pilot, close your eyes
    in sleep, Toroa?

On your way to your home-ground at Otakou Heads
    you tried to rest briefly on the Wai-o-te-mata
    but were shot at by ignorant people.
    Crippled, you found a resting-place at Whanga-nui-a-Tara;
    found space at last to recompose yourself. And now

    without skin and flesh to hold you together
    the division of your aerodynamic parts lies whitening
    licked clean by sun and air and water. Children will
    discover narrow corridors of airiness between, the suddenness
    of bulk. Naked, laugh in the gush and ripple – the play
    of light on water.

You are not alone, Toroa. A taniwha once tried to break out
    of the harbour for the open sea. He failed.
    He is lonely. From the top of the mountain nearby he calls
    to you: Haeremai, haeremai, welcome home, traveller.

Your head tilts, your eyes open to the world.

                                             Hone Tuwhare (1986)

21

On the Random Distribution of King Parrots

for Harold Bloom

Clustered in a mallee ash, swinging upside down
and exposing the red heart of confidence, these
      Blue Mountain king parrots
behave according to their listing in *Slater's
Australian Field Guide.* Surveying the apparent
      wealth of wet sclerophyll
      forest, they remain high
in the grey deadwood. Indigenous and content,
even the threat of diminishing habitat

fails to dislodge them. Once, I saw a pair of king
parrots where they should not have been. It was between
      Wandering and Williams.
They were feeding on a corrugated gravel
road with a small flock of regent parrots – *smokies*
      as we call them back home.
      It was sultry weather
and the moisture suggested the colours of each

species ran like waterpaint over the yellow

grain spilled from the backs of loosely tarped trucks. Stephen

      said he had seen a few

around over the years. The farmer at Happy

Valley reckoned they'd have escaped from aviaries.

      Driving home on the same

         road I found the remnants

of a flock of *smokies*, hit en masse by a fast-

travelling vehicle. In the centre, one orange

heart was exposed, its partner nowhere to be seen.

      The landscape I come from

is often perceived as *surreal*: but it's the sound

of a chainsaw as it tears into mallee ash,

      an orange symphony

         of king parrots straining

to make itself heard high overhead, that is more

surreal than anything I've seen or heard back there.

                                            John Kinsella (1998)

22

The Camel Comes to Us from the Barbarians

This one is enormous: rough-cut,
the fur like matted felt –
and so much of it,

rising in vulgar mounds upon its back
as if the sand itself had belched
into heaven's beard. Gods,

what malevolence! The eye a constant
rolling orb, glistening with ill intent,
yellowed, gummed with hair, more hairs

than you or I would care to count,
that eye marks every move its jailer makes
and waits for him to step too near –

one blow would cripple any man.
Another specimen stands bellowing
beneath the farthest palm. Though slighter,

The Camel Comes to Us from the Barbarians

it daunts equally, staked haunches
straining, muscles potent as the reek
that saturates our sun-baked marketplace.

About the larger one some purpose lurks:
Hindquarters splayed, it tugs against its ropes,
snorts, yearns its massive head and slavers

toward that godawful sound. Could
the drabber one be female, and its mate?
More monsters in our midst!

And yet . . . if these vile creatures be
like geese, or dogs, and their offspring
learn to cuddle the one

who coddles them first – why,
our fortune's pegged for sure.
Let us display our sternest countenance,

then apportion what they most desire
according to the measure of their service.
A rare commodity, these beasts –

who cannot know
what beauty wreaks, what mountains
pity moves.

Rita Dove (1999)

23

Frog

If it could be done, would you want
to be made into a frog?
If it meant having a thin-boned spine,
gray-green humid skin that feels
the sting of any slight insect you might
otherwise gobble and swallow,
sit the world apart
in a wide, four-legged sweaty squat,
the beating of your heart showing in your throat,
and yet be able to leap
a distance many times your own measure.

If it meant you can enter water
more vast than your body can ever swim through and,
nevertheless relaxed, arms and legs stretched open,
like a molecule afloat,
round eyes absorbing the world
through greenish inner screens that draw
towards and within you
the soft slithering silk of the water's surface,

the slosh and sway of high palm leaves,

defiant birds gathered in the immense blue and,

even then, still be able to stare at the sun.

And if it also meant you could dive deep in the far depth of the water,

go down, down to where there is no bottom, none to feel or reach,

down to an infinity of movement that requires no breath.

If it could be done and it meant you would

know love, would you come,

to be born a Man? Or even, woman?

Marilène Phipps (2007)

from *Endless Inter-States*

They go down to the expressways, baskets
In hand, they go down with rakes, shovels
And watering cans, they go down to pick

Beans and trim tomato plants, they go down
In wide-brimmed hats and boots, passing
By the glass-pickers, the Geiger counters, those

Guarding the toxic wastes. They go down
Remembering the glide of automobiles, the
Swelter of children in back seats, pinching, twitching,

Sand in their bathing suits, two-fours of Molson's
In the trunk of the car. They go down, past
The sifters, the tunnellers, those who transport

Soil from deep in the earth, and are content
To have the day before them, are content to imagine
Futures they will inhabit, beautiful futures

from Endless Inter-States   24

Filled with unimagined species, new varieties of
Plant life, sustainable abundance,
An idea of sufficient that is global. Or,

Because cars now move on rails underground,
The elevated roads are covered in earth,
Vines drape around belts of green, snake

Through cities, overgrown and teeming
With grackles and rats' nests, a wall
Of our own devising, and the night

Watchmen with their machine guns
Keeping humans, the intoxicated,
Out. I am sorry for this version, offer

You coffee, hot while there is still
Coffee this far north, while there is still news
To wake up to, and seasons

Vaguely reminiscent of seasons.

                                    Sina Queyras (2009)

25

The Whale

That January, the sea brought us a message –
Monumental, big as a black bus, ribbed,
Rubbery, vulcanised, arched like a bridge,

There it lay one morning – a sperm whale,
Making for another world, and perished.

It looked old as the rock. It was mottled brick-red
And chalked pinkish-white, like a fresco
In a dark church. Its fluke was etched

Delicately greenish-pink; its side
Rose, a black slag-heap, a hill of cinders,
Red oxides, oily residues and clinker.

We were drawn to it. Huddled on the bank-top,
Facing the horizon, hunched against the wind
And cold, we stared and stared at it, in wonder.

Then the sea, with the noise of a great machine,
Rolled its dark bulk towards us and, graceful
As weed, it raised one flipper like a sign;

And the sea heaved; lifted its great weight, light
As a breath, or a gift – Here, take it.

Katrina Porteous (2014)

26

Fox

I heard a cough
as if a thief was there
outside my sleep
a sharp intake of air

a fox in her fox-fur
stepping across
the grass in her black gloves
barked at my house

just so abrupt and odd
the way she went
hungrily asking
in the heart's thick accent

in such serious sleepless
trespass she came
a woman with a man's voice
but no name

as if to say: it's midnight
and my life
is laid beneath my children
like gold leaf

                                        Alice Oswald (2016)

#ExtinctionRebellion

The day will come when papers
will only tell leaf-stories
of blackbirds' quarrels with sparrows.

Their pages will roll back into trees
and the front page will be bark.

Tabloids will be hundred-winged birds
singing earth anthems.

I'll settle into the buttress root of my armchair
and watch ants swarm

to text me secrets from the soil
adding emojis
of all our lost species.

I'll be surrounded by phones
that light up with chlorophyll,
vibrating like workers in their hives –

an apiary of apps.

I'll touch a vanda orchid
and it'll open
easily as hypertext,

everyone will hold leaves
intently as smartphones

to hear them retweet birdsong
from archives.

This is my homepage, where I belong.
This is my wood wide web,

my contour map
with which to navigate
a new internet –

rootlets sparking towards rootlets
underground.

Underground
where resistance is in progress –

fungal friends working in darkness,
their windows blacked out.

Pascale Petit (2020)

28

The Sun Wanders, Searching for Shade

In the beginning of time
the buildings in my village
did not bear fruit, grow or expand.
Only the farmland, the sirissa
and guinea peach trees grew and multiplied.

Yet in three decades there has been
an explosion of fruitfulness.
Stones and soil have copulated
to give birth to walls and roofs,
high rise dwellings, a forest of buildings.

These houses have no front yards
or entrance ways. There are no murungai
trees flowering by the back door.
The wind can find no mango or neem
leaves to gather. There are no branches
for the crows to cry from.

The Sun Wanders, Searching for Shade

The houses have borne fruit, spreading out

with a sigh. What used to contain two floors

now rise higher and higher, until

they tear at the sky. The coconut trees,

defeated, bend their heads low.

The parrots which had desired

the cashew and the many sparrows,

losing all sense of direction

head towards the open wilderness.

The woodpecker searching for dead trees

breaks into pillars of granite.

The few surviving siris and guinea peach trees

shed their newly formed fruit and the last

of their flowers, and stand in solitude.

The water is drying at their roots.

In a village parched of trees

the sun wanders, searching for shade.

Alari (2005); Shash Trevett (translated 2021)

29

Whale

After a sculpture by Dentsu Jayme Syfu at Naic, Phillippines, May 2017

Rolled half onto its back	this assemblage of slabby muscle
chucked up by the tide	blubber, jaw and tongue
stiff flukes rucked	beating heart
in sand, in surf which laps	transmitting into the wide
and sings –	its steady signal – bell
slant pectoral fin	a metronome
beginning to unravel, huge maw:	rising through green walls of cold
an overturned	belly-hull
dump truck – clutter of buckets	three hundred thousand pounds
take-out Styrofoam	clanging cage of ribs
toys bright as fish	and room-sized lungs
sun prisms through polypropylene	sighing gust, drawn-out brontide
tangle of cables	to span the gyres
this keel	echoing
black plastic	down a thousand miles
stitched up with twine	blue-dark
fishing line, snarled in the	sea lanes. Mouth – too little of a word
shape of	a revolving door, a lobby hung
hide loosening	with keratin, frayed
in places	baleen brooms that sweep
sloughing false skin	the swells

Whale 29

shucking	mouthful by mouthful
wave-stirred	the ballast
rising chemical stink	of krill, half a million spinning slivers
as summer bakes	crimson and silver
to warp and blister	gorge the bloat
the arched back simmers. Across the sand	the pungent load
burst bin-bags spill	what is sieved and swilled
like purge fluid –	a strained deluge
the great grooved throat	waterfalls back into the sea
inflates	the boom and thrash
in hoax	of flukes
of vigorous decay	thruster blades
from the inside out –	to haul it away.

Cindy Botha (2022)

30

The Year of One Thousand Fires

Early in the spring,
hiking along the coast,
we spot the charred remains
of a giant oak tree,

its hollowed trunk roomier
than most apartments. It is illegal
to sleep here, it is illegal
to be homeless here

and so the poor reside
in rusty RVs at the foot
of this billion-dollar view.
The headline in the newspaper insists:

'America will never be socialist,'
as if that had ever been in doubt …
Everywhere the rapacious harvesting of resources,
but scarcity reigns supreme. Everywhere a resurgent

love for one's country, but no faith
in the meaning of government. Everywhere a newfound
love of God, but a concurrent deadening of the soul.
All day, I read about the Gracchi,

Cato, Casca, Cassius and all night,
I dream of Brutus's final letter to Cicero
before falling on his sword at Philippi.
'Did we wage war to destroy despotism,

or to negotiate the terms of our bondage?'
We have recorded the sound
the wind makes on Mars, but we cannot
listen to one another … All year we binge-watch

an endless rerun of the past. Eighty years
after Guernica, another coup in Catalonia and for
the first time in history, the brightest objects in the sky
are all artificial. A year after Woolsey,

wild mustard returns to carpet the hills,
its fire-resistant flowers bursting out of their sooty stasis.
There will be no hibernation for us,
no sleep except our final slumber.

André Naffis-Sahely (2022)

PART 2

People and Places

The Garden

How vainly men themselves amaze
To win the Palm, the Oke, or Bayes;
And their uncessant Labours see
Crown'd from some single Herb or Tree.
Whose short and narrow vergèd Shade
Does prudently their Toyles upbraid;
While all Flow'rs and all Trees do close
To weave the Garlands of repose.

Fair quiet, have I found thee here,
And Innocence thy Sister dear!
Mistaken long, I sought you then
In busie Companies of Men.
Your sacred Plants, if here below,
Only among the Plants will grow.
Society is all but rude,
To this delicious Solitude.

No white nor red was ever seen
So am'rous as this lovely green.
Fond Lovers, cruel as their Flame,
Cut in these Trees their Mistress name.

Little, Alas, they know, or heed,
How far these Beauties Hers exceed!
Fair Trees! where s'eer your barkes I wound,
No Name shall but your own be found.

When we have run our Passions heat,
Love hither makes his best retreat.
The *Gods*, that mortal Beauty chase,
Still in a Tree did end their race.
Apollo hunted *Daphne* so,
Only that She might Laurel grow.
And *Pan* did after *Syrinx* speed,
Not as a Nymph, but for a Reed.

What wond'rous Life in this I lead!
Ripe Apples drop about my head;
The Luscious Clusters of the Vine
Upon my Mouth do crush their Wine;
The Nectaren, and curious Peach,
Into my hands themselves do reach;
Stumbling on Melons, as I pass,
Insnar'd with Flow'rs, I fall on Grass.

Mean while the Mind, from pleasure less,
Withdraws into its happiness:
The Mind, that Ocean where each kind
Does streight its own resemblance find;
Yet it creates, transcending these,
Far other Worlds, and other Seas;
Annihilating all that's made
To a green Thought in a green Shade.

31   The Garden

Here at the Fountains sliding foot,
Or at some Fruit-trees mossy root,
Casting the Bodies Vest aside,
My Soul into the boughs does glide:
There like a Bird it sits, and sings,
Then whets, and combs its silver Wings;
And, till prepar'd for longer flight,
Waves in its Plumes the various Light.

Such was that happy Garden-state,
While Man there walk'd without a Mate:
After a Place so pure, and sweet,
What other Help could yet be meet!
But 'twas beyond a Mortal's share
To wander solitary there:
Two Paradises 'twere in one
To live in Paradise alone.

How well the skilful Gardner drew
Of flow'rs and herbes this Dial new;
Where from above the milder Sun
Does through a fragrant Zodiack run;
And, as it works, th' industrious Bee
Computes its time as well as we.
How could such sweet and wholsome Hours
Be reckon'd but with herbs and flow'rs!

Andrew Marvell (1681)

32

from *Trivia*

      But hark! Distress with screaming Voice draws nigh'r,
And wakes the slumb'ring Street with Cries of Fire.
At first a glowing Red enwraps the Skies,
And born by Winds the scatt'ring Sparks arise;
From Beam to Beam, the fierce Contagion spreads;
The spiry Flames now lift aloft their Heads,
Through the burst Sash a blazing Deluge pours,
And splitting Tiles descend in rattling Show'rs.
Now with thick Crouds th' enlighten'd Pavement swarms,
The Fire-man sweats beneath his crooked Arms,
A leathern Casque his vent'rous Head defends,
Boldly he climbs where thickest Smoak ascends;
Mov'd by the Mother's streaming Eyes and Pray'rs,
The helpless Infant through the Flame he bears,
With no less Virtue, than through hostile Fire,
The *Dardan* Hero bore his aged Sire.
See forceful Engines spout their levell'd Streams,
To quench the Blaze that runs along the Beams;
The grappling Hook plucks Rafters from the Walls,
And Heaps on Heaps the smoaky Ruine falls.
Blown by strong Winds the fiery Tempest roars,
Bears down new Walls, and pours along the Floors:

32 from Trivia

The Heav'ns are all a-blaze, the Face of Night
Is cover'd with a sanguine dreadful Light;
'Twas such a Light involv'd thy Tow'rs, O *Rome*,
The dire Presage of mighty *Cæsar*'s Doom,
When the Sun veil'd in Rust his mourning Head,
And frightful Prodigies the Skies o'erspread.
Hark! the Drum thunders! far, ye Crouds, retire:
Behold! the ready Match is tipt with Fire,
The nitrous Store is laid, the smutty Train
With running Blaze awakes the barrell'd Grain;
Flames sudden wrap the Walls; with sullen Sound,
The shatter'd Pile sinks on the smoaky Ground.
So when the Years shall have revolv'd the Date,
Th' inevitable Hour of *Naples*' Fate,
Her sap'd Foundations shall with Thunders shake,
And heave and toss upon the sulph'rous Lake;
Earth's Womb at once the fiery Flood shall rend,
And in th' Abyss her plunging Tow'rs descend.

John Gay (1716)

33

from *The Deserted Village*

Seats of my youth, when every sport could please,
How often have I loitered o'er thy green,
Where humble happiness endeared each scene;
How often have I paused on every charm,
The sheltered cot, the cultivated farm,
The never-failing brook, the busy mill,
The decent church that topped the neighbouring hill,
The hawthorn bush, with seats beneath the shade,
For talking age and whispering lovers made.
How often have I blessed the coming day,
When toil remitting lent its turn to play,
And all the village train, from labour free,
Led up their sports beneath the spreading tree,
While many a pastime circled in the shade,
The young contending as the old surveyed;
And many a gambol frolicked o'er the ground,
And sleights of art and feats of strength went round.
And still as each repeated pleasure tired,
Succeeding sports the mirthful band inspired;
The dancing pair that simply sought renown,
By holding out to tire each other down;
The swain mistrustless of his smutted face,

33   from The Deserted Village

    While secret laughter tittered round the place;
The bashful virgin's sidelong looks of love,
The matron's glance that would those looks reprove.
These were thy charms, sweet village; sports like these,
With sweet succession, taught even toil to please;
These round thy bowers their cheerful influence shed,
These were thy charms – But all these charms are fled.

    Sweet smiling village, loveliest of the lawn,
Thy sports are fled and all thy charms withdrawn;
Amidst thy bowers the tyrant's hand is seen,
And desolation saddens all thy green:
One only master grasps the whole domain,
And half a tillage stints thy smiling plain:
No more thy glassy brook reflects the day,
But, choked with sedges, works its weedy way.
Along thy glades, a solitary guest,
The hollow-sounding bittern guards its nest;
Amidst thy desert walks the lapwing flies,
And tires their echoes with unvaried cries.
Sunk are thy bowers in shapeless ruin all,
And the long grass o'ertops the mouldering wall;
And trembling, shrinking from the spoiler's hand,
Far, far away, thy children leave the land.

    Oliver Goldsmith (1770)

from *In Memoriam*

VII

Dark house, by which once more I stand
      Here in the long unlovely street,
      Doors, where my heart was used to beat
So quickly, waiting for a hand,

A hand that can be clasp'd no more –
      Behold me, for I cannot sleep,
      And like a guilty thing I creep
At earliest morning to the door.

He is not here; but far away
      The noise of life begins again,
      And ghastly thro' the drizzling rain
On the bald street breaks the blank day.

Alfred, Lord Tennyson (1850)

35

I Saw Red Evening Through the Rain

I saw red evening through the rain,
Lower above the steaming plain;
I heard the hour strike small and still,
From the black belfry on the hill.

Thought is driven out of doors to-night
By bitter memory of delight;
The sharp constraint of finger tips,
Or the shuddering touch of lips.

I heard the hour strike small and still,
From the black belfry on the hill.
Behind me I could still look down
On the outspread monstrous town.

The sharp constraint of finger tips
Or the shuddering touch of lips,
And all old memories of delight
Crowd upon my soul to-night.

I Saw Red Evening Through the Rain 35

Behind me I could still look down

On the outspread feverish town;

But before me still and grey

And lonely was the forward way.

                                          Robert Louis Stevenson (written 1875)

36

from *Our Casuarina Tree*

Like a huge Python, winding round and round
        The rugged trunk, indented deep with scars
        Up to its very summit near the stars,
A creeper climbs, in whose embraces bound
        No other tree could live. But gallantly
The giant wears the scarf, and flowers are hung
In crimson clusters all the boughs among,
        Whereon all day are gathered bird and bee;
And oft at nights the garden overflows
With one sweet song that seems to have no close,
Sung darkling from our tree, while men repose.

When first my casement is wide open thrown
        At dawn, my eyes delighted on it rest;
        Sometimes, and most in winter, – on its crest
A gray baboon sits statue-like alone
        Watching the sunrise; while on lower boughs
His puny offspring leap about and play:
And far and near kokilas hail the day;
        And to their pastures wend our sleepy cows;
And in the shadow, on the broad tank cast
By that hoar tree, so beautiful and vast,
The water-lilies spring, like snow enmassed.

Toru Dutt (1876)

37

Fair Weather

This level reach of blue is not my sea;
Here are sweet waters, pretty in the sun,
Whose quiet ripples meet obediently
A marked and measured line, one after one.
This is no sea of mine, that humbly laves
Untroubled sands, spread glittering and warm.
I have a need of wilder, crueler waves;
They sicken of the calm, who knew the storm.

So let a love beat over me again,
Loosing its million desperate breakers wide;
Sudden and terrible to rise and wane;
Roaring the heavens apart; a reckless tide
That casts upon the heart, as it recedes,
Splinters and spars and dripping, salty weeds.

Dorothy Parker (1928)

Glory

This same evening that I write I witnessed,
Resting on a garden bench and looking westward,
Sublime splendours.

Beyond the blood-red rose-engarrisoned footpath,
And in the dun green flatlands where a few human lights glimmered,
Wild indigo and magenta rainstorms invested
The dark recesses of the mountain ranges.

Clouds overhead burst into cornelian flames,
Transmuting by their strange flow all the garden pigments.
Then was revealed, in a dim turquoise interstice,
A very young, remote, and slender, but outshining,
But all predominant moon.

In such an hour the soul finds an appeasement
Not justified by reasons of commonsense.
In that hour she asks of the inscrutable
No more petulant questions.

Mary Ursula Bethell (1929)

39

Deep in the Hills

Once I thought the land I had loved and known
Lay curled in my inmost self; musing alone
In the quiet room I unfolded the folded sea,
Unlocked the forest and the lonely tree,
Hill and mountain valley beach and stone,
All these, I said, are here and exist in me.

But now I know it is I who exist in the land;
My inmost self is blown like a grain of sand
Along the windy beach, and is only free
To wander among the mountains, enter the tree,
To turn again a sea-worn stone in the hand,
Because these things exist outside of me.

O far from the quiet room my spirit fills
The familiar valleys, is folded deep in the hills.

Ruth Dallas (1953)

Angola

I was not born from your womb
but I loved you each Spring
with the exuberance of a seed …

I was not born from your womb
but in you I buried
my longings
and suffered the storm
of a flower transplanted
prematurely …

I was not born from your womb
but I drank your charm
in nights of transparent
poetry …

I was not born from your womb
but under your shadow
I fertilized new offsprings
and opened my arms
to a transcendent destiny …

Angola,
you will not be the land of my birth
but you are the land of my womb.

    Amélia Veiga (1963); Gerald Moore (translated 1984)

41

O Earth

I have laid them
my dead
in the gentleness of your loved breasts
there where the waterfalls wash the feet
of the cliffs
Keep them
o earth
keep in the folds of your clay
keep the bones of my brothers.

Often in the evening
I shall go and weep for them there
at the hour when the heart
draws arpeggios
across the koras
of dream.

And if one day the wind of liberty
came breathing after me
on your mountains and dunes
your rivers and plains
o earth

let it cradle

and rock

my brothers

heroes whose flesh was torn

and who are dead that liberty might live.

    Siriman Cissoko (1966); John Reed and Clive Wake (translated 1972)

42

The Sash Window

Outside that house, I stood like a dog;
The window was mysterious, with its big, dull pane
Where the mud pastes are thrown by dark, alkaline skies
That glide slowly along, keeping close to the ground.

– But for the raging disgust which shook me
So that my throat was scratched by her acid
(Whose taste is the true Latin of culture) –
I could have lived the life of these roads.

That piece of filthy laurel moves up and down,
And then the dead rose-leaves with their spat-on look
Where the sour carbon lies … under
The sash of the window comes the smell of stewing innards,

With the freshly washed lavatory – I know where
The old linoleum has its platinum wet patches
And the disinfectant dries off in whiffs.
Hellish, abominable house where I have been young!

With your insane furnishings – above all
The backs of dressing-tables where the dredged wood
Faces the street, raw. And the window
With its servant-maid's mystery, which contains *nothing*,

Where I bowed over the ruled-up music books
With their vitreous pencilling, and the piano keys
That touched water. How forlornly my strong, destructive head
Eats again the reek of the sash window.

Rosemary Tonks (1967)

The Echoes

Over the vast summer hills
I shall commission the maternal sun
To fetch you with her long tilted rays,

The slow heave of the valleys
Will once again roll the hymns of accompaniment
Scattering the glitter of the milky way over the bare fields.

You will meet me
Underneath the shadow of the timeless earth
Where I lie weaving the seasons.

You will indulge in the sway dances of your kin
To the time of symphonic flutes
Ravishing the identity of water lilies.

I have opened the mountain gates
So that the imposing rim
Of the Ruwenzori shall steal your image.

Even the bubbling lips of continents
(To the shy palms of Libya)
Shall awake the long-forgotten age.

The quivering waters of the Zambezi river
Will bear on a silvery blanket your name
Leading it to the echoing of the sea.

Let me not love you alone
Lest the essence of your being
Lie heavy on my tongue
When you count so many to praise.

Mazisi Kunene (1982)

44

Londoners

We huddled on street corners
Coughing like hags
Feet suffocating in great big leathers
Rooted in muck and slime
The smoke from our cigarette butts
Escaping into the already scented air
And finding freedom amongst its friends
The unmistakable aroma of urine and uncleanliness.
Where once our skin had known the softness of youth
Now lay chunks of flesh
Taut and fibrous
Stretching like used twine
As it built a wall against wind and cold
Our noses twitched;
Trembling lips went dry; unsmiling
We looked into each other's eyes where pain lay
Silent and cold;
Someone belched
And released a load of last night's merriment
Last evening we had known bliss in pubs
And in the morning light;
Souls loitering in weary bodies

We held each other close

And looked to the approaching bus

Which we scrambled into

Our jeans scrubbing in the metal railings

Till we found solace in the upper deck

Where herds of cattle might have passed on sand.

We peered through the dust for seats

And there stretched our legs and laughed

For we knew not how death haunted us

Such was the gift of civilisation!

                                                Kristina Rungano (1984)

An Old Colonial Building

1

Through sunlight and shadow dust swirls,
through the scaffolding raised-up around
the colonial edifice, over the wooden planks
men live on to raise it brick by brick, the imperial
image of it persisting right down, sometimes,
to the bitter soil in the foundation, sometimes finding, too,
the noble height of a rotunda, the wide, hollow corridors
leading sometimes to blocked places, which, sometimes,
knocked open, are stairs down to ordinary streets.

2

Down familiar alcoves sometimes brimming
with blooms sometimes barren I go to xerox
glancing at the images caught in the circular pond,
now showing the round window in the cupola as duckweed drifting,
day and night caught in the surface, no longer textbook
clean, but murky, the naive goldfish searching
mindlessly around in it, shaking the pliant lotus stems
and the roots feeling for earth, swirling orange and white,
gills opening and leeching, in and out of the high window bars.

3

Might all the pieces of ruins put together present
yet another architecture? Ridiculous the great heads on money,
laughable the straight faces running things. We pass in this corridor
in the changing surface of the pond by chance
our reflections rippling a little. We'd rather not bend;
neither of us is in love with flags or fireworks.
So what's left are these fragmentary, unrepresentative words,
not uttered amidst the buildings of chrome and glass, but beside
a circular pond riddled with patterns of moving signs.

Leung Ping-Kwan (1986); Gordon T Osing (translated 1992)

Perhaps the World Ends Here

The world begins at a kitchen table. No matter what, we must eat to live.

The gifts of earth are brought and prepared, set on the table. So it has been since creation, and it will go on.

We chase chickens or dogs away from it. Babies teethe at the corners. They scrape their knees under it.

It is here that children are given instructions on what it means to be human. We make men at it, we make women.

At this table we gossip, recall enemies and the ghosts of lovers.

Our dreams drink coffee with us as they put their arms around our children. They laugh with us at our poor falling-down selves and as we put ourselves back together once again at the table.

This table has been a house in the rain, an umbrella in the sun.

Wars have begun and ended at this table. It is a place to hide in the shadow of terror. A place to celebrate the terrible victory.

We have given birth on this table, and have prepared our parents for burial here.

At this table we sing with joy, with sorrow. We pray of suffering and remorse. We give thanks.

Perhaps the world will end at the kitchen table, while we are laughing and crying, eating of the last sweet bite.

Joy Harjo (1994)

47

My Aunts Don't Want to Move

They hug their house around them
half-underground in a deafening city,
hurry across the yellow courtyard
with its waxy plants and coverless bed
where no one sleeps, sweats and turns
by doors to secret, sombre rooms.

Their house contracts and holds them.
Its simple brocade sitting-room
where uncle, father, brother preside –
they face each other on the mantelshelf.
The Alpine picture, the dividing curtain
women draw when unknown men appear.

They revolve their house before them.
It turns itself inside out.
The ancient wiring, knee-high stoves,
continuous stream of delicacies,
the bruising bangles waiting in the drawer –
just visible on the brink of the world.

Moniza Alvi (2000)

48

Map Store

Imagine him coming back from a war –
one of those wars that happen elsewhere,
from which some people return with memories enough
to make a film that almost feels realistic –
coming back, as I say, from a desert in North Africa
and opening, with his newfound expertise in thirst,
a juice stand.
He was dropping some ice into those freshly-squeezed
beverages which became at the end of the forties
an emblem of the new Pax Americana
when he discovered water puddling under the cooler.
He imagined a sea, a mainland, an island
and in this way there grew within him
the vague idea of what geography is.
Later, a grandson who had never been to war
converted the juice stand into a map store.

If you pass by it some day
on a blocked artery in the heart of Manhattan
you'll see people who aren't from here
coming and going and rarely buying anything.
I once saw a woman brush some dust off a mountain
and a girl trail one of her braids over a lake
and I heard one man try to describe to another

the location of his distant house in a distant village close to a distant city
which appeared as a tiny dot on the map of his distant country.

I pass by this place
not to share these strangers' griefs
nor to pour water into the Nile, which appears as a motionless snake
on the picture that hangs facing the door,
nor even to contemplate the aura that must have been there
just above the right knee of the store's original owner
whom I now see in a portrait wearing his uniform and medals
but with no sign of his wooden leg
and no trace of the water that leaked from his cooler.

Truly, I don't know why I pass by this place
but I can see now with my own eyes
the map seller
terrified, perhaps for the first time,
living through a war he had no time to sign up for –
because this time the war came to him.

Iman Mersal (2006); Robyn Creswell (translated 2022)

49

Under These Stones

This is the spot where the walls stood:
my father's father's house
destroyed by fire
where the smell of beet-red coffee berries filled the air
and the smoke went up in silence.

The house I visited, the year
my father could not bring his father back,
is now either a memory or this brambled pit,
the footpath to it overrun by leaf-of-life
whose stems we'd strip to make stick dolls.

Now, under these scorched foundation stones,
lies the unstirred clay steeped in grandfather's life:
a life I never knew.
No photograph from which to root his face –
yet his nearness throbs
in the richness of a September noon.

49   Under These Stones

       Every memory must break somewhere –
       the air palpable with the grace of a drinking hen
       strutting to its nest with a promise to fulfill,
       the clucking in the shadow of banana leaves
       that glistened with morning dew –
       no telling what time was or where it went –
       the days replete with trees to climb.

                                     Delores Gauntlett (2007)

50

Nomad in the Sunset

This time he fell in the abyss on his horse, and the Sun fell with him

And his voice never reached us again,

Only a stone inscription remained.

Where was the army headed in a whirlwind,

The raging Saks and Hunnus.

From far ends of Asia they flew over to this end

Horsemen of the boundless Universe.

The whirlpool of stars within their reach,

Offspring of steppe winds and mountain winds.

Life force of flesh sapped by the distance,

Last drop of water stolen by scorching sands.

At times, the tamed eagle would fall in the hands of the enemy

Life passing away in the saddle

Leaving the pensive nomad to grieve, resting sorrowful head on his fingers:

Oh how narrow the paths of this material existence.

I played qomuz, filled with sadness: I had thought I was strong

But the spinning Earth with me on it, turned out to be smaller than the eye of a needle.

I heard many tales of death, every battle rushing towards tasting it

The space of the spinning Universe where I dwelt, shrinking to just my existence.

50   Nomad in the Sunset

Everything in this world is fleeting, all things pass

– the land was divided, the flocks and soul ripped away from me

In the emptiness of the steppe, luring far off fires burned,

As I rode impetuously at lightning speed, the reigns of destiny no longer in my hand,

Suddenly not realising: have I been pierced by light or the searing heat of the sword?

What far reaches … where would my tribe go now?

Where would it go, where to aim in darkness?

My small clan, that split off from the big tribe

Flung up in a moment like a spark off a horseshoe

The Sun falls into the wound of my heart

Maybe I didn't know that this world's colour is the colour of blood,

like the sunset.

Now I release my soul to be

And my steed, closer than my soul,

I release him too. Be free.

Roza Mukasheva (2008); Hamid Ismailov (translated 2012)

51

Leaving Fingerprints

I know this frosted landscape
better than it knows itself, its layers
a busy clock of history, still ticking.

Under my feet I feel the trail of the slug,
the snail, the earth's deep squirm
around an anklet or an amulet, a broken cup.

Lost, the names of the ones
whose fingers made and used
and threw away these things,

written and rewritten in the calligraphy
of roots. The worm's heave
and turn delivers messages up,

scribbled in folds of soil and mud, afterthoughts
that grow to trees, trunks with arms,
branches with fingers, twigs with nails,

51   Leaving Fingerprints

    scratches on air, tear
    after tear on a white page.
    These names have given their artefacts away

    to be sparse as winter. Here I am, they say.
    Here and here for you to see,
    fingerprinted on the sky.

Imtiaz Dharker (2009)

52

The Ruin

after the Anglo-Saxon

What walls and gables, wonders still of workmanship.
Whoever's stronghold this was, havoc's jumbled it
beyond all mending, uprooting towers, rusting together tools.
What was built by strange smiths, skilled in stone,
is burst, underdug, eaten down by age: weird bricks
litter this wasteground. And what of the wrights
and hammer-men, the mortar-mixers and heavers
of slab? A long time laid off, fast in the earth,
while their sons passed, and the sons of their sons
knew no like work. But these walls withstood
mosses and snows, the fall of kings, peace's
indifferent wear by rain and rubbing kine.
Magogs raised them. Their wit matched their might.
Their great halls gawped. Their tile floors gleamed
with muscle girls and monster fish. Here
springs were housed, and happiness found haven
among men making merry, their shadows merging,
nimble as a change of mind, massive on the inner walls.
What happened? Ruin already had root. Plague came, within

and without. No one, however high, whatever wit,
was spared. Here, wide open to the wind, is where
breath was fought for, where men raved. Now birdsong
embroiders space among the rubble of what stood.
And the builders are broken down, bone by bone,
mindless and muddled together in the bottomless muck.
Half-recalled by these grim, rain-collecting courts,
by this unshattered span of arch, this blush of broken slate,
are those who twisted gold, empearled pins and gazed
on heaps of gems that beat and sparked. Houses were here.
Hot water sprang from wells and the walls held
vaults of steam and banked beds of embers, like precious stones.
Frost could get no grip. But all such days are gone.

Jacob Polley (2012)

53

Till

I've known exposed till, soft ground returning

footsteps with a sprung rhythm. I've scaled spoil

and scree, running upwards against churning,

slipping stone, defiant over the shale-oil

lacquered slopes. Round-calved, I've laboured sand dunes,

trod for miles over sinking bog, weary,

tired, but happy all the same. Whistled tunes

when the sun was full and rubbed at bleary,

sleep-filled eyes in long hours idled with friends.

The winter wash is clearing the moraine.

I've set up home, alone, almost content,

with walls for old memories; the telephone

asleep in its cradle. The sills have silted.

I'm living at an angle now, stilled, tilted.

Gregor Addison (2013)

54

I Pick Up My Footprints

I stoop to pick up my footprints,

somebody seeing me might think

I'm gathering mushrooms,

healing herbs,

or flowers into a bunch,

but no –

I collect my footprints,

my traces everywhere

I walked for many years:

Here are the footprints I left while herding sheep on the steppe.

Here, I took this path to school,

and these are my steps from my route to work.

'I'm gathering my footprints here

so that strangers don't trample them,'

I tell anyone who's curious.

(Epiphany:

a footprint is –

a symbol, by definition, of:

'something rooted in the past')

I Pick Up My Footprints

In my mind, I slip my footprints
between the pages –
now whenever I read a book,
I chance upon an old footprint:
I study it for a long time,
the footprint I left as a child
walking beneath a cherry tree.

All the footprints gathered so far,
an entire footstep herbarium in books –
if I put them all in one row,
their path wouldn't lead me home.

    Vasyl Holoborodko (2015); Svetlana Lavochkina (translated 2016)

55

Sentinel

Five forty-four am is not morning,
no matter what Swede lightbulbs teach.
Too far to tell tinnitus from cricket,
racket from reach.
too late to believe in witches,
too early
to feel
brand new.
It is the best time to admit: I
am unsure of what I do.
I know my post.
Have been on patrol most of the night
keeping watch for the arrival of something
more train than thought.
Soon, you nine-to-fiver
swallowing your sen-suh-ble habits,
will leave through the sliding doors of a heart murmur,
shutting open
a dream coming through the wrong chamber.
Sometimes, always, a stranger sitting next to you,
you,

mindful of the wide gap,
welcoming different mornings
with different needs.
But we're not so different.
We also have stomachs to feed.

Jennifer Anne Champion (2016)

56

Grandmothers Abroad

You will see them pacing platform tracks,
at corner stores, and in the park,
pushing kids about in prams,
always first to get on board.
You will see them walk the dog,
pretending to be nonchalant
about the plastic bags
they've got tied around their hands.
You will see them at markets
in pursuit of perfect fruits,
taking breaks on city benches
in saris and salwar suits.
You will see them luxuriate
in cricket scores and royal scandals,
at the bus-stop with the shopping,
edging home in socks and sandals.

You will see them, then you won't.
The plumage of their sari tails
devoured by hues of black and grey,
the outwardness of Kanchivaram
not quite right for mid-sized Durham.

You will see them scourged of colour,

bandaged in their daughter's fleeces,

hounded by their sons and nieces

to put away the jewellery pieces.

You will want to tell them to resist,

at least, the flaccid slacks and pumps that wait,

the visits to the Oxfam shops.

Granny, don't become that omnipresent

migrant woman, stripped of all her memories.

Find a courtyard filled with sun

and let your gold relentlessly

unfold upon the paisley sleeves

of your bereaved imaginings.

Tishani Doshi (2018)

Paradise

Is Paradise an island of perfection?
The reward for a life of good deeds,
a payment to the virtuous?
The antidote to hell's fire and brimstone
and endless suffering?
Will there be white sands and crystalline waters,
all pina coladas, swimsuits, shades and sun beds,
our bones finally relaxing in their sun-soaked skins?
Will we see storms far out at sea
that mysteriously never trouble our shores?
And after years in this perfect land,
will we not secretly long for a night
when we wake to skies of bruised clouds,
lightning, a deluge of rain
and a murder of crows
scything the fat-faced acned moon.

Roger Robinson (2019)

House

This poem is like a house where I once lived.
Upstairs, four rooms where everyone I loved
lay and dreamt their solitary dreams,
the sound of crying in the turquoise bathroom,
the tap's fat drip. Above our heads, an attic
with a splintered window, spongy dust, bare brick,
a battered trunk that held an ocean,
another of shame, and from the rafters,
rain and rain and rain.
      Downstairs, a different weather –
four muggy rooms, the telly's sunny blether,
a technicolor garden. I hopped the path
on my red space hopper, and raised my hand
to wave at a girl who looked like me, upstairs,
her hands and face pressed tightly to the glass.

Hannah Lowe (2021)

Knots

Blushed with blood and false summits, outcast,
    I keep a familiar distance. Without wind cheats

or the right shoes, I have words with mountains.
    Accent bending in the wind, I eke aloud

Wordsworth's *Gipsies*, the lines hung over me
    hawk-like, as his cloud-double slips the Screes

toward Appleby. Our luck lands blackly there too.
    He saw us as spots, a spectacle, knots.

The same fight picked in private fields.
    Is it time to move on? Let me sit this stone

on the marker's pile. Tell the capital I am a Traveller
    under open sky and yes, our bonfire's still raging.

Jo Clement (2022)

Touchstone

This is the only way for the mind
to wander: firmly balanced against the hoe
rooted in the earth, grounded
in the province of my fields.

The soil warms to my feet. I am based
in reality. Cannot stray too far become
a cloud dreamer. The grains of wood
score calendars in my hands.

My brown world below is stronger than
cloud in the blue.
Though the mind aches to know
the hand gripping a tool says: this is.

When passing birds tug at
my lifeline my head lifts. My feet
refuse to yield. The moment gone my life
goes slack again. Only my eyes water.

Olive Senior (2022)

PART 3

Play

61

Gratiana Dancing and Singing

See! with what constant Motion
Even, and glorious, as the Sun,
   Gratiana steers that Noble Frame,
Soft as her breast, sweet as her voice
That gave each winding Law and poise,
   And swifter than the wings of Fame.

She beat the happy Pavement
By such a Star made Firmament,
   Which now no more the Roof envies;
But swells up high with *Atlas* ev'n
Bearing the brighter, nobler Heav'n,
   And in her, all the Deities.

Each step trod out a Lovers thought
And the Ambitious hopes he brought,
   Chain'd to her brave feet with such arts;
Such sweet command, and gentle awe,
As when she ceas'd, we sighing saw
   The floor lay pav'd with broken hearts.

So did she move; so did she sing
Like the Harmonious spheres that bring
    Unto their Rounds their music's aid;
Which she performed such a way,
As all th' enamoured world will say
    The *Graces* danced, and *Apollo* play'd.

Richard Lovelace (1649)

from *Ode for Musick on St Cecilia's Day*

Descend ye Nine! descend and sing;
      The breathing Instruments inspire,
Wake into Voice each silent String,
      And sweep the sounding Lyre!
      In a sadly-pleasing Strain
      Let the warbling Lute complain:
         Let the loud Trumpet sound,
         Till the Roofs all around
         The shrill Ecchos rebound:
    While in more lengthen'd Notes and slow,
The deep, majestick, solemn Organs blow.
      Hark! the Numbers, soft and clear,
      Gently steal upon the Ear;
      Now louder, and yet louder rise,
      And fill with spreading Sounds the Skies;
Exulting in Triumph now swell the bold Notes,
In broken Air, trembling, the wild Musick floats;
      Till, by degrees, remote and small,
        The Strains decay,
        And melt away
      In a dying, dying Fall.

from Ode for Musick on St. Cecilia's Day

By Musick, Minds an equal Temper know,
    Nor swell too high, nor sink too low.
If in the Breast tumultuous Joys arise,
Music her soft, assuasive Voice applies;
    Or when the Soul is press'd with Cares
    Exalts her in enlivening Airs.
Warriors she fires with animated Sounds;
Pours Balm into the bleeding *Lover*'s Wounds:
    Melancholy lifts her Head;
    Morpheus rowzes from his Bed;
        Sloath unfolds her Arms and wakes;
        List'ning *Envy* drops her Snakes;
Intestine War no more our *Passions* wage,
And giddy *Factions* hear away their Rage.

                        Alexander Pope (1713)

from *The Art of Dancing*

Now see prepared to lead the sprightly dance,
The lovely nymphs, and well-dressed youths advance;
The spacious room receives each jovial guest,
And the floor shakes with pleasing weight oppressed:
Thick ranged on every side, with various dyes
The fair in glossy silks our sight surprise;
So, in a garden bathed with genial showers,
A thousand sorts of variegated flowers,
Jonquils, carnations, pinks, and tulips rise,
And in a gay confusion charm our eyes.
High o'er their heads, with numerous candles bright,
Large sconces shed their sparkling beams of light,
Their sparkling beams, that still more brightly glow
Reflected back from gems, and eyes below:
Unnumbered fans to cool the crowded fair,
With breathing zephyrs move the circling air;
The sprightly fiddle, and the sounding lyre,
Each youthful breast with generous warmth inspire;
Fraught with all joys the blissful moments fly,
Whilst music melts the ear, and beauty charms the eye.
    Now let the youth, to whose superior place
It first belongs the splendid ball to grace,

With humble bow, and ready hand prepare,

Forth from the crowd to lead his chosen fair;

The fair shall not his kind request deny,

But to the pleasing toil with equal ardour fly.

      But stay, rash pair, nor yet untaught advance,

First hear the muse, ere you attempt to dance:

By art directed o'er the foaming tide,

Secure from rocks the painted vessels glide;

By art the chariot scours the dusty plain,

Springs at the whip, and hears the straightening rein;

To art our bodies must obedient prove,

If e'er we hope with graceful ease to move.

Soame Jenyns (1729)

64

from *The Paper Kite*

    The kite, completed thus, is borne along
By some blest leaders of the shining throng,
Who to the fields elate with joy repair,
And wait the blast that wafts her in the air.
    So when some new-built ship is launched for sail,
And only tarries for the prosp'rous gale,
Th' impatient crew each rising breeze explore,
And long to see her sail, and quit the shore.
    Now from the central string extends the line,
And for the flight lie harnessed rolls of twine.
This takes the string, remote his partner stands,
And holds the kite, impatient, in his hands.
She tugs to go; he scarce without a prayer
Commits the struggling engine to the air.
But oh! what passions fluctuate in his mind,
To whom th' important office is consigned,
To whom 'tis giv'n to steer the rising kite,
Pilot her motions, and assist her flight!
Soon as she mounts, he flying meets the wind,
Oft chides his mate, and often looks behind.
The trickling twine glides through his glowing hand,
And joy transporting flushes all the band;

from The Paper Kite 64

Applauding shouts pursue her as she flies,
And raise the wind that bears her to the skies.
So larks on poisèd pinions soar sublime,
In ether lost, still singing as they climb.

Samuel Bowden (1733)

65

from *Cricket. An Heroic Poem*

When the returning sun begins to smile,
And shed its glories round this sea-girt isle;
When newborn nature, decked in vivid green,
Chases dull winter from the charming scene;
High-panting with delight, the jovial swain
Trips it exulting o'er the flow'r-strewed plain.
Thy pleasures, Cricket! all his heart control;
Thy eager transports dwell upon his soul.
He weighs the well-turned bat's experienced force
And guides the rapid ball's impetuous course;
His supple limbs with nimble labour plies,
Nor bends the grass beneath him as he flies.
The joyous conquests of the late-flown year,
In fancy's paint, with all their charms appear,
And now again he views the long-wished season near.
O thou, sublime inspirer of my song,
What matchless trophies to thy worth belong!
Look round the globe, inclined to mirth, and see
What daring sport can claim the prize from thee!
    Not puny Billiards where, with sluggish pace,
The dull ball trails before the feeble mace;

from Cricket. An Heroic Poem

Where no triumphant shouts, no clamours, dare
Pierce through the vaulted roof and wound the air,
But stiff spectators quite inactive stand,
Speechless attending to the striker's hand;
Where nothing can your languid spirits move,
Save where the marker bellows out 'Six-love!',
Or when the ball, close-cushioned, slides askew,
And to the op'ning pocket runs, a *cou*!
Nor yet that happier game, where the smooth Bowl
In circling mazes wanders to the goal;
Where, much divided between fear and glee,
The youth cries 'Rub! – O flee, you ling'rer, flee!'

    Not Tennis' self, thy sister sport, can charm,
Or with thy fierce delights our bosoms warm:
Though full of life, at ease alone dismayed,
She calls each swelling sinew to her aid,
Her echoing courts confess the sprightly sound,
While from the racket the brisk balls rebound.
Yet, to small space confined, ev'n she must yield
To nobler Cricket the disputed field.

    O parent Britain, minion of renown!
Whose far-extended fame all nations own,
Of sloth-promoting sports, forewarned, beware!
Nor think thy pleasures are thy meanest care.
Shun with disdain the squeaking masquerade,
Where fainting Vice calls Folly to her aid;
Leave the dissolving song, the baby dance,
To soothe the slaves of Italy and France.
While the firm limb and strong-braced nerve are thine,
Scorn eunuch sports, to manlier games incline,

65   from Cricket. An Heroic Poem

    Feed on the joys that health and vigour give;
Where Freedom reigns, 'tis worth the while to live.
        Nursed on thy plains, first Cricket learned to please,
And taught thy sons to slight inglorious ease:
And see where busy counties strive for fame,
Each greatly potent at this mighty game!
Fierce Kent, ambitious of the first applause,
Against the world combined asserts her cause;
Gay Sussex sometimes triumphs o'er the field,
And fruitful Surrey cannot brook to yield;
While London, queen of cities! proudly vies,
And often grasps the well-disputed prize.

James Dance (1744)

66

from *The Prelude*

And in the frosty season, when the sun
Was set, and, visible for many a mile,
The cottage-windows through the twilight blazed,
I heeded not the summons: happy time
It was indeed for all of us; for me
It was a time of rapture! Clear and loud
The village-clock tolled six – I wheeled about,
Proud and exulting like an untired horse
That cares not for his home. – All shod with steel
We hissed along the polished ice, in games
Confederate, imitative of the chase
And woodland pleasures, – the resounding horn,
The pack loud-chiming, and the hunted hare.
So through the darkness and the cold we flew,
And not a voice was idle: with the din
Smitten, the precipices rang aloud;
The leafless trees and every icy crag
Tinkled like iron; while far-distant hills
Into the tumult sent an alien sound
Of melancholy, not unnoticed while the stars,
Eastward, were sparkling clear, and in the west
The orange sky of evening died away.

William Wordsworth (1805)

from *Andromeda*

[...] afar, like a dawn in the midnight,
Rose from their seaweed chamber the choir of the mystical sea-maids.
Onward toward her they came, and her heart beat loud at their coming,
Watching the bliss of the gods, as they wakened the cliffs with their laughter.
Onward they came in their joy, and before them the roll of the surges
Sank, as the breeze sank dead, into smooth green foam-flecked marble,
Awed; and the crags of the cliff, and the pines of the mountain were silent.

Onward they came in their joy, and around them the lamps of the sea-nymphs,
Myriad fiery globes, swam panting and heaving; and rainbows
Crimson and azure and emerald, were broken in star-showers, lighting
Far through the wine-dark depths of the crystal, the gardens of Nereus,
Coral and sea-fan and tangle, the blooms and the palms of the ocean.

Onward they came in their joy, more white than the foam which they scattered,
Laughing and singing, and tossing and twining, while eager, the Tritons
Blinded with kisses their eyes, unreproved, and above them in worship
Hovered the terns, and the seagulls swept past them on silvery pinions
Echoing softly their laughter; around them the wantoning dolphins
Sighed as they plunged, full of love; and the great sea-horses which bore them
Curved up their crests in their pride to the delicate arms of the maidens,

from Andromeda 67

Pawing the spray into gems, till a fiery rainfall, unharming,
Sparkled and gleamed on the limbs of the nymphs, and the coils of the mermen.
    Onward they went in their joy, bathed round with the fiery coolness,
Needing nor sun nor moon, self-lighted, immortal [...]

Charles Kingsley (1858)

from *A Swimmer's Dream*

V

A dream, a dream is it all – the season,
    The sky, the water, the wind, the shore?
A day-born dream of divine unreason,
    A marvel moulded of sleep – no more?
For the cloudlike wave that my limbs while cleaving
Feel as in slumber beneath them heaving
Soothes the sense as to slumber, leaving
    Sense of nought that was known of yore.

A purer passion, a lordlier leisure,
    A peace more happy than lives on land,
Fulfils with pulse of diviner pleasure
    The dreaming head and the steering hand.
I lean my cheek to the cold grey pillow,
The deep soft swell of the full broad billow,
And close mine eyes for delight past measure,
    And wish the wheel of the world would stand.

The wild-winged hour that we fain would capture
    Falls as from heaven that its light feet clomb,
So brief, so soft, and so full the rapture
    Was felt that soothed me with sense of home.

To sleep, to swim, and to dream, for ever –
Such joy the vision of man saw never;
For here too soon will a dark day sever
    The sea-bird's wing from the sea-wave's foam.

A dream, and more than a dream, and dimmer
    At once and brighter than dreams that flee,
The moment's joy of the seaward swimmer
    Abides, remembered as truth may be.
Not all the joy and not all the glory
Must fade as leaves when the woods wax hoary;
For there the downs and the sea-banks glimmer,
    And here to south of them swells the sea.

Algernon Charles Swinburne (1889)

69

The Blind Musician

The vesper bells rang out the day
    The jostling crowd moved on its way:
The sexton flared the old church light;
    The lamps were lit and all was bright.
Then slowly thro' the open door,
    The moving crowd began to pour;
And smiling youth and hoary age,
    Alike were crowding round the stage.
A blind musician, flushed and gay,
    Mounted the stage and picked his way
To where an old piano lone
    Awaited to adjust its tone.
His form swayed as moved by the breeze,
    Electric fingers swept o'er the keys,
And like the mighty tides of the sea
    That slowly swell and flood the lea,
He made the strains of music rise
    And swell till they had lashed the skies.
The crowd sat mute, their minds had flown
    On trembling notes to shores unknown,
Belated teamsters left their dray
    And toward the chapel sought their way;

The Blind Musician

A star peeped thro' the clouds o'er head
    And seemed to trip and onward sped.
The blind musician lower bent,
    And swift the rolling music went
Like the gentle ebb and the flow
    Of ocean tides that come and go,
Or like the roll of drum and fife,
    Or sounds of conflict and of strife,
E'en more, the mocking bird would trill
    Its warbling lays and all was still
Till soft the sound of winds swept o'er,
    And broke a mighty tempest roar.
Lightening seemed in the player's hand;
    A music cyclone struck the land.
Then came a creak as if were struck
    Some massive house, or trees were plucked
From their roots, and the thunder's might
    Made those near by leap up in fright
Then came the lull, the storm was gone:
    The musician seemed sad and lone.
Thought he must of his darling wife,
    Whom he'd ne'er seen in all his life,
But as he sat in sad repose,
    Much he looked like the last fair rose.
Tho' music vibrated ev'ry vein,
    A rose bloomed out on Sharon's plain.
O, what genius in deed and thought!
    What mechanism by heaven wrought!
A soul of light, tho' earth and skies
    Gave not light to his blinded eyes,

69   The Blind Musician

    His fingers sought the keys once more,
      And played he then as ne'er before
    And tossed he like a ship on the main,
      Till his soul echoed the last sad strain.

James T Franklin (1900)

70

Untitled

As if words were not enough,
The *theta* and *iota* of a Greek flute –
Unsculptural, unaccountable –
Matured, laboured, crossed frontiers.

It's impossible to forsake the flute:
It can't be stopped with clenched teeth,
It can't be prodded into speech with the tongue,
It can't be kneaded with the lips.

The flute player doesn't know repose –
It seems to him that he's alone,
That some time or other out of lilac clay
He formed his native sea.

With the urgency of recollecting lips,
With an ambitious, resonant murmur,
He collects the sounds to save them,
Neatly, stingily.

70   Untitled

Later we shall not be able to repeat him,
Clods of clay in the sea's hands,
And when I am filled with the sea
My measure has become disease.

My own lips now lisp,
Plague or murder at the root.
And involuntarily falling, falling,
I diminish the force of the flute.

Osip Mandelstam (1937); James Greene (translated 1978)

when faces called flowers float out of the ground

when faces called flowers float out of the ground
and breathing is wishing and wishing is having –
but keeping is downward and doubting and never
 – it's april(yes,april;my darling)it's spring!
yes the pretty birds frolic as spry as can fly
yes the little fish gambol as glad as can be
(yes the mountains are dancing together)

when every leaf opens without any sound
and wishing is having and having is giving –
but keeping is doting and nothing and nonsense
 – alive;we're alive,dear:it's(kiss me now)spring!
now the pretty birds hover so she and so he
now the little fish quiver so you and so i
(now the mountains are dancing,the mountains)

when more than was lost has been found has been found
and having is giving and giving is living –
but keeping is darkness and winter and cringing
 – it's spring(all our night becomes day)o,it's spring!
all the pretty birds dive to the heart of the sky
all the little fish climb through the mind of the sea
(all the mountains are dancing;are dancing)

E E Cummings (1950)

72

Song

Song closed up the air,
    space contracted all about,
walls of song on every side,
    a roof of sound above.

I had a book of poetry
    within my music-prison,
poetry from Wales
    that would not let me in at first:

for worthless chatter
    swarmed into all I thought,
but song switched off the worldly talk
    within the wireless of my ear.

A burden of song weighed on me,
    I had a book of poetry nearby,
and took in my embrace
    a little feminine rhyme,

and mouth to mouth I kissed
    that mouth from Wales,
and music swarmed on music,
    music raining into music.

With a sod of my mind
    and a sod from Wales,
I'll make a turf-stack of the air,
    a beehive cell within the song.

        Seán Ó Ríordáin (1952); Frank Sewell (translated 2014)

73

In Georgia

I loafed about at leisure munching pears
and bathing every morning in the sea,
drinking my khvanchkara in the bazaar,
bright shirt, felt hat; a small woman
for whom I spoilt her summer holiday.
Beneath the oleanders and beneath
the hollyhocks my boring persecutions.
A few painters wandering with palettes,
the yoghourt-seller shouting in the dawn,
and high up in the hillside restaurant
the nightfall violins scraping their strings.
From there the road struggling and weaving
and suddenly crunching on tiny stones,
twisting, rearing up, and at last
clear from the mountains and their humming voice
drops like a waterfall.
In the silent village morning
the gates playing like children,
and the old man with the silver head
leaving his piles of hay to open them.
They took us arm in arm. It was movement,
it was crisp chickens, wine a dark glimmer,

the peaches glowing softly while I ate,

emptied the horn, and dropped it on the table:

I in the Russian way dancing and weeping

to songs I am unable to translate.

She hardly trembling in her string of pearls,

lowering her shy head, the small woman

looking at me who did not know me.

Again the journey.

Among plane trees, among ivy.

Cracking green walnuts, each of us

searching with our eyes for the sea.

And I whitened my lips with pressing them,

drew my ribs tight and wept invisibly.

The coast came forward and the sea with it.

Yevgeny Yevtushenko (1956); Robin Milner-Gullard and Peter Levi (translated 1962)

74

The Day Lady Died

It is 12:20 in New York a Friday
three days after Bastille day, yes
it is 1959 and I go get a shoeshine
because I will get off the 4:19 in Easthampton
at 7:15 and then go straight to dinner
and I don't know the people who will feed me

I walk up the muggy street beginning to sun
and have a hamburger and a malted and buy
an ugly NEW WORLD WRITING to see what the poets
in Ghana are doing these days
                                      I go on to the bank
and Miss Stillwagon (first name Linda I once heard)
doesn't even look up my balance for once in her life
and in the GOLDEN GRIFFIN I get a little Verlaine
for Patsy with drawings by Bonnard although I do
think of Hesiod, trans. Richmond Lattimore or
Brendan Behan's new play or *Le Balcon* or *Les Nègres*
of Genet, but I don't, I stick with Verlaine
after practically going to sleep with quandariness

and for Mike I just stroll into the PARK LANE
Liquor Store and ask for a bottle of Strega and

then I go back where I came from to 6th Avenue
and the tobacconist in the Ziegfeld Theatre and
casually ask for a carton of Gauloises and a carton
of Picayunes, and a NEW YORK POST with
                                          her face on it

and I am sweating a lot by now and thinking of
leaning on the john door in the 5 SPOT
while she whispered a song along the keyboard
to Mal Waldron and everyone and I stopped breathing

                                          Frank O'Hara (1959)

Allegro

After a black day, I play Haydn,
and feel a little warmth in my hands.

The keys are ready. Kind hammers fall.
The sound is spirited, green, and full of silence.

The sound says that freedom exists
and someone pays no taxes to Caesar.

I shove my hands in my haydnpockets
and act like a man who is calm about it all.

I raise my haydnflag. The signal is:
'We do not surrender. But want peace.'

The music is a house of glass standing on a slope;
rocks are flying, rocks are rolling.

The rocks roll straight through the house
but every pane of glass is still whole.

Tomas Tranströmer (1962); Robert Bly (translated 2001)

76

The Joy of Writing

Why does this written doe bound through these written woods?
For a drink of written water from a spring
whose surface will xerox her soft muzzle?
Why does she lift her head; does she hear something?
Perched on four slim legs borrowed from the truth,
she pricks up her ears beneath my fingertips.
Silence – this word also rustles across the page
and parts the boughs
that have sprouted from the word 'woods.'

Lying in wait, set to pounce on the blank page,
are letters up to no good,
clutches of clauses so subordinate
they'll never let her get away.

Each drop of ink contains a fair supply
of hunters, equipped with squinting eyes behind their sights,
prepared to swarm the sloping pen at any moment,
surround the doe, and slowly aim their guns.

76 The Joy of Writing

They forget that what's here isn't life.
Other laws, black on white, obtain.
The twinkling of an eye will take as long as I say,
and will, if I wish, divide into tiny eternities,
full of bullets stopped in mid-flight.
Not a thing will ever happen unless I say so.
Without my blessing, not a leaf will fall,
not a blade of grass will bend beneath that little hoof's full stop.

Is there then a world
where I rule absolutely on fate?
A time I bind with chains of signs?
An existence become endless at my bidding?

The joy of writing.
The power of preserving.
Revenge of a mortal hand.

Wisława Szymborska (1967); Stanisław Barańczak and
Clare Cavanagh (translated 1995)

77

Untitled

And now at the end of the round
he bends over the ropes,
hit hard he goes down,
the giant, first worked over
on the inside,
skillfully and doggedly,
pounded in the face, pummeled in all his flesh:
and there the shouting cavea,
struck by its own
sudden dumbness,
springs up, fixes
on him a single
terrifying pupil, glares at him,
accursed stare,
there on the mat,
until he's counted out,
mercilessly out.
                        And the other
still clenched
in his relaxing guard,
still caught in the web

77   Untitled

of the interrupted fight – around him
quivers a halo
of unappeased strength – he is there
alone, left
balancing on the black undertow,
close to falling
downward, into the dark deposit
of sweat and drivel, into the teeming hell
of unexpressed violence …
he is finished too, finished both of them,
created by the struggle,
undone by its break up, hard and sudden.

Mario Luzi (1985); Luigi Bonaffini (translated 1992)

78

Swimming after Thoughts

In memoriam: Robert Penn Warren

Across the blackened pond and back again,
he's swimming in an ether all his own;

lap after lap, he finds the groove
no champion of motion would approve,

since time and distance hardly cross his mind
except as something someone else might find

of interest. He swims and turns, making
his way through frogspawn, lily pads, and shaking

reeds, a slow and lofty lolling stroke
that cunningly preserves what's left to stoke

his engines further, like a steamwheel plunging
through its loop of light. He knows that lunging

only breaks the arc of his full reach.
He pulls the long, slow oar of speech,

addressing camber-backed and copper fish;
the minnows darken like ungathered wishes,

flash and fade – ideas in a haze of hopes
ungathered into syntax, sounding tropes.

The waterbugs pluck circles round his ears
while, overhead, a black hawk veers

to reappraise his slithering neck and frogs
take sides on what or who he is: a log

or lanky, milk-white beast. He goes on swimming,
trolling in the green-dark glistening

silence and subtending mud where things
begin, where thoughts amass in broken rings

and surface, break to light, the brokered sound
of lost beginnings – fished for, found.

Jay Parini (1990)

79

Bouncing Boy

(for Paul)

All the squares of trampoline are taken
by children leaping like chessmen
who won't play the game. Up, flying.
from tiny freeholds, hitting the sky's
elastic surprise, then down.

There's a space for you always.
Two kids eating ice-cream
with careful darts of the tongue
watch as you start to climb
the icy November sky, hand over hand.

You hear the clap of the sea
and your bright blue trampoline applauding
with the dull fervour of rubber
each time you go down,

79   Bouncing Boy

      and the kids eating ice-cream
      with wind in their teeth say nothing
      as the time mounts and your turn
      grows impossibly long.

                                     Helen Dunmore (1999)

80

Captain of the Lighthouse

The late hour trickles to morning. The cattle low profusely by the anthill where brother and I climb and call Land's End. We are watchmen overlooking a sea of hazel-acacia-green, over torrents of dust whipping about in whirlwinds and dirt tracks that reach us as firths.

We man our lighthouse – cattle as ships. We throw warning lights whenever they come too close to our jagged shore. The anthill, the orris-earth lighthouse, from where we hurl stones like light in every direction.

Tafara stands on its summit speaking in *sea-talk*, Aye-aye me lad – a ship's a-coming! And hurls a rock at the cow sailing in. Her beefy hulk jolts and turns. Aye, Captain, another ship saved! I cry and furl my fingers into an air-long telescope – searching for more vessels in the day-night.

Now they low on the anthill, stranded in the dark. Their sonorous cries haunt through the night. Aye, methinks, me miss my brother, Captain of the lighthouse, set sail from land's end into the deepest seventh sea.

Togara Muzanenhamo (2006)

Lightness

As I climb the slope with the sledge in tow
clouds gather; the sky turns grey.
I see light prints of a hare in snow.

Far down on the shore below
a whale lies still at the edge of the bay.
I climb the slope with the sledge in tow.

At the brow of the hill I brace then let go –
runners scatter ice in a crystal spray.
I follow light prints of a hare in snow.

Out on the skyline, prow towards Faroe,
a container ship slips along the seaway.
I climb the slope with the sledge in tow.

On the coast beyond Hoy, lying low,
the puffball globe of Dounreay.
The prints of the hare are lost in snow.

Lightness

My feet fall heavy and deep and slow –
the sky is like lead; the sea turns grey.
I climb the slope with the sledge in tow
seeking light prints of a hare in snow.

Yvonne Gray (2007)

Pier

Speak to our muscles of a need for joy.
W H Auden, 'Sonnets from China' (XVII)

Left at the lodge and park, snout to America.
Strip to togs, a shouldered towel, flip-flop over
the tarmac past the gangplanked rooted barge,
two upended rowboats and trawlers biding time.
Nod to a fisherman propped on a bollard,
exchange the weather, climb the final steps
up to the ridge. And then let fly. Push wide,
tuck up your knees so the blue nets hold you,
wide-open, that extra beat. Gulp cloud;
fling a jet trail round your neck like a feather boa,
toss every bone and sinew to the plunge.
Enter the tide as if it were nothing,
really nothing, to do with you. Kick back.
Release your ankles from its coiled ropes;
slit water, drag it open, catch your breath.
Haul yourself up into August. Do it over,
raucously. Head first. This time, shout.

Vona Groarke (2009)

Common\wealth

at the Commonwealth Institute, London

Without wheels their boy bodies are eloquent
in the cool air, tightly coiled springs
that jump and whirl and oscillate effortlessly

the same way boasts slip off
the roofs of their mouths like clay shingles.
Each move is demonstrated

with familiar ease, every element of motion
executed like a locksmith decodes
a knot, then the ringing chatter settles

like a dropped coin,

the expectant clatter of skateboards
rises then turns to air, flared jeans
lift, then fall, as though for a second

83   Common\wealth

    they had lungs, and the boys are mounted.
    The first boy's feet propel him
    towards idle boasts and after graceful

    coasting, he launches himself, a raised flag;
    his flight is jerky yet hopeful, like a plea
    in a tongue he hasn't mastered the rolling of.

Nii Ayikwei Parkes (2012)

84

Prologue (Grime Mix)

Harry 'Bells' Bailey

When my April showers me with kisses
I could make her my missus or my mistress
but I'm happily hitched – sorry home girls –
said my vows to the sound of the Bow Bells
yet her breath is as fresh as the west wind,
when I breathe her, I know we're predestined
to make music; my muse, she inspires me,
though my mind's overtaxed, April fires me,
how she pierces my heart to the fond root
till I bleed sweet cherry blossom en route
to our bliss trip; there's days she goes off me,
April loves me not; April loves me
with a passion, dear doctor, I'm wordsick
and I got the itch like I'm allergic
but it could be my shirt's on the cheap side;
serenade overnight with my peeps wide,
nothing like her, liqueur, an elixir,
overproof that she serves as my sick cure,
she's as strong as a ram, she is Aries,

84 Prologue (Grime Mix)

see my jaw-dropping jeans, she could wear these;
see my jaw dropping neat Anglo-Saxon,
I got ink in my veins more than Caxton
and it flows hand to mouth, here's a mouthfeast,
verbal feats from the streets of the South-East
but my April, she blooms every shire's end,
fit or vint, rich or skint, she inspires *them*
from the grime to the clean-cut iambic,
rime royale, rant or rap, get your slam kick
on this Routemaster bus: get cerebral
Tabard Inn to Canterbury Cathedral,
poet pilgrims competing for free picks,
Chaucer Tales , track by track, here's the remix
from below-the-belt base to the topnotch;
I won't stop all the clocks with a stopwatch
when the tales overrun, run offensive,
or run clean out of steam, they're authentic
cos we're keeping it real, remember this:
Chaucer Tales were an unfinished business.
May the best poet lose, as the saying goes.
May the best poet muse be mainstaying those
on the stage, on the page, on their subject:
me and April, *we're* The Rhyming Couplet
I'm The Host for tonight, Harry Bailey,
if I'm tongue-tied, April will bail me,
I'm MC but the M is for mistress
when my April shows me what a kiss is . . .

Patience Agbabi (2015)

85

Handfast

For K M Grant

She is away.
The feathers in my eye spoke outwards.
She is the accident that happens.
The sun bursts hazel on my shoulders.
She is the point of any sky.

Come here, here, here:
if it's a tree you'd sulk in, I am pine;
if earth, I'm risen terracotta;
if it's all to air you'd turn, turn to me.
You are flying inside me.

Seventy times her weight,
I stand fast.
My hand is blunt and steady.
She is fierce and sure:
lands, scores, punctures the gloveskin.

85 Handfast

And why I asked
for spirals stitched where she might perch:
fjord blue, holm green, scarlet, sand,
like her bloodline, Iceland to Arabia:
because her hooded world's my hand –

Vahni Capildeo (2016)

Girl in the Blue Pool

Years back and full of echoes.
Chlorine, urine, raucous
Cuff of voices on broken surface.
A boy on the edge rowdily teeters
And you, knees flexed, arms back
Are on the pulse of your stroke. Suppose
It is you, now, in the pink bikini, close
To making five hundred metres
As the ceiling splinters with echoes.

Suppose you touch the tiles on the turn
And vanish. The churn
Of bubbles streams at your heels
While you shake water out of your ears
To catch the voice of your instructor
Who paces you, outpaces you
On the blue-wet tiles. How her voice echoes.
You should not be wearing a bikini
And you were slow on the turn.

86   Girl in the Blue Pool

I am years back and full of echoes.
The silver stream where you swim
Has long ago been swallowed,
But at your temples the lovely hollows
Play in June light. Suppose
There is one length left in you, knees flexed
Arms back. Chlorine, urine, raucous
Voices on shattered surface. If that boy topples
You too will go down.

Helen Dunmore (2017)

87

The Kite

    At last it lifts.
        It leaves
The turf that had no more to offer it,
        And drifts
        Above the eaves
With every trace of ground-devotion quit.

    Backtrack. Bounce back. Held in
By thread, simplicity on wings,
It rumples, thick and thin
        Against its bones,
        And structure sings
        As it disowns
The fiddliness and pinionedness of Earth,
        In soft rebirth.

    It is a kite,
        A kit
For getting airborne in pursuit of joy,
        A sight
        Designed to fit
By being both a triumph and a toy.

87   The Kite

    Yet flight is just one answer
    To finding Earth a sapped domain.
    Swivel and see! A dancer
        Shimmies across
        A sunny plain,
        And all the loss
From time's interminable fade-to-grey
        Is blown away.

                        Andrew Wynn Owen (2018)

88

Huia

I was the first of birds to sing
I sang to signal rain
the one I loved was singing
and singing once again

My wings were made of sunlight
my tail was made of frost
my song was now a warning
and now a song of love

I sang upon a postage stamp
I sang upon your coins
but money courted beauty
you could not see the joins

Where are you when you vanish?
Where are you when you're found?
I'm made of greed and anguish
a feather on the ground

+

88   Huia

>I lived among you once
>and now I can't be found
>I'm made of things that vanish
>a feather on the ground

Bill Manhire (2020)

89

Sea: Night Surfing in Bolinas

Maybe enough light • to score a wave • reflecting moonlight, sand • reflecting moonlight and you • spotting from shore • what you see only • as silhouette against detonating bands • of blue-white effervescence • when the crown of the falling • swell explodes upward • as the underwave blows through it • a flash of visibility quickly • snuffed by night • the surf fizzling and churning • remitting itself to darkness • with a violent stertor • in competition with no other sounds

paddling through dicey backwash • the break zone of • waist-high NW swell • as into a wall of obsidian • indistinguishable from night sky • diving under, paddling fast • and before I sit • one arm over my board • I duck and • listen a moment underwater • to the alien soundscape • not daytime's clicks and whines of • ship engines and sonar • but a low-spectrum hum • the acoustic signature of fish, squid, • crustaceans rising en masse • to feed at the surface I feel • an eerie peacefulness veined with fear

after twenty minutes the eyes • adjust, behind the hand dragging through water • bioluminescent trails • not enough light • to spot boils • or flaws in nearing • waves appear even larger • closing-in fast • then five short strokes into a dimensionless • peeler, two S-shaped turns, the • kick out, and from shore • your shout

89   Sea: Night Surfing in Bolinas

it is cowardice that turns my eyes • from the now-empty beach • for with you I became • aware of an exceptional chance • I don't believe in • objective description, only • this mess, experience, the perceived • world sometimes shared • in which life doesn't • endure, only • the void endures • but your vitality stirred it • leaving trails of excitation • I've risen from the bottom of • myself to find • I exist in you • exist in me and • against odds I've known even rapture, • rare event, • which calls for • but one witness

Forrest Gander (2021)

How to Perfect a Flip Turn

The first thing to remember about flip turns
is that they are made blind. Don't look ahead

to the wall or to your legs. Trust that
for once your body will not fight itself,

trust that grace comes easy as breathing.
It's a delicious thrill, darting through water

& your whole self jonesing
with chlorine want & for once your limbs

perfectly long & lean & your body caught
in its own headlong momentum.

The moment before the turn is like
opening a window to unexpected birdsong

despite rain and the late hour. It is never
wanting for anything except the easy slip

of your body in its spandex skin.
You kick off wherever your feet land.

Cynthia Miller (2021)

PART 4

Relationships

Sonnet 106

When in the chronicle of wasted time
I see descriptions of the fairest wights,
And beauty making beautiful old rhyme
In praise of ladies dead and lovely knights,
Then, in the blazon of sweet beauty's best,
Of hand, of foot, of lip, of eye, of brow,
I see their antique pen would have express'd
Even such a beauty as you master now.
So all their praises are but prophecies
Of this our time, all you prefiguring;
And, for they look'd but with divining eyes,
They had not skill enough your worth to sing;
    For we, which now behold these present days,
    Have eyes to wonder, but lack tongues to praise.

William Shakespeare (1609)

92

On My First Son

Farewell, thou child of my right hand, and joy;
My sin was too much hope of thee, loved boy,
Seven years thou wert lent to me, and I thee pay,
Exacted by thy fate, on the just day.
O, could I lose all father, now. For why
Will man lament the state he should envy?
To have so soon 'scap'd world's, and flesh's rage,
And, if no other misery, yet age!
Rest in soft peace, and, asked, say here doth lie
Ben Jonson his best piece of poetry.
For whose sake, henceforth, all his vows be such,
As what he loves may never like too much.

Ben Jonson (1616)

93

The Bait

Come live with me, and be my love,
And we will some new pleasures prove
Of golden sands, and crystal brooks,
With silken lines, and silver hooks.

There will the river whispering run
Warmed by thy eyes, more than the sun.
And there the'enamoured fish will stay,
Begging themselves they may betray.

When thou wilt swim in that live bath,
Each fish, which every channel hath,
Will amorously to thee swim,
Gladder to catch thee, than thou him.

If thou, to be so seen, be'st loth,
By sun, or moon, thou darkenest both,
And if myself have leave to see,
I need not their light, having thee.

The Bait

Let others freeze with angling reeds,
And cut their legs, with shells and weeds,
Or treacherously poor fish beset,
With strangling snare, or windowy net:

Let coarse bold hands, from slimy nest
The bedded fish in banks out-wrest,
Or curious traitors, sleavesilk flies
Bewitch poor fishes' wandering eyes.

For thee, thou need'st no such deceit,
For thou thyself art thine own bait,
That fish, that is not catched thereby,
Alas, is wiser far than I.

John Donne (1633)

94

To His Coy Mistress

Had we but World enough, and Time,
This coyness Lady were no crime.
We would sit down, and think which way
To walk, and pass our long Loves Day.
Thou by the *Indian Ganges* side
Should'st Rubies find: I by the Tide
Of *Humber* would complain. I would
Love you ten years before the Flood:
And you should if you please refuse
Till the Conversion of the *Jews*.
My vegetable Love should grow
Vaster than Empires, and more slow.
An hundred years should go to praise
Thine Eyes, and on thy Forehead Gaze.
Two hundred to adore each Breast:
But thirty thousand to the rest.
An Age at least to every part,
And the last Age should show your Heart.
For Lady you deserve this State;
Nor would I love at lower rate.
    But at my back I alwaies hear
Times winged Charriot hurrying near:

And yonder all before us lye
Desarts of vast Eternity.
Thy Beauty shall no more be found;
Nor, in thy marble Vault, shall sound
My ecchoing Song: then Worms shall try
That long preserv'd Virginity:
And your quaint Honour turn to dust;
And into ashes all my Lust.
The Grave's a fine and private place,
But none I think do there embrace.

    Now therefore, while the youthful hew
Sits on thy skin like morning dew,
And while thy willing Soul transpires
At every pore with instant Fires,
Now let us sport us while we may;
And now, like am'rous birds of prey,
Rather at once our Time devour,
Than languish in his slow-chapt pow'r.
Let us roll all our Strength, and all
Our sweetness, up into one Ball:
And tear our Pleasures with rough strife,
Thorough the Iron gates of Life.
Thus, though we cannot make our Sun
Stand still, yet we will make him run.

                                    Andrew Marvell (1681)

95

To the Ladies

Wife and servant are the same,
But only differ in the name:
For when that fatal knot is tied,
Which nothing, nothing can divide:
When she the word obey has said,
And man by law supreme has made,
Then all that's kind is laid aside,
And nothing left but state and pride:
Fierce as an Eastern prince he grows,
And all his innate rigour shows:
Then but to look, to laugh, or speak,
Will the nuptial contract break.
Like mutes she signs alone must make,
And never any freedom take:
But still be governed by a nod,
And fear her husband as a God:
Him still must serve, him still obey,
And nothing act, and nothing say,
But what her haughty lord thinks fit,
Who with the power, has all the wit.

Then shun, oh! shun that wretched state,
And all the fawning flatt'rers hate:
Value your selves, and men despise,
You must be proud, if you'll be wise.

Lady Mary Chudleigh (1703)

96

First Love

I ne'er was struck before that hour
    With love so sudden and so sweet,
Her face it bloomed like a sweet flower
    And stole my heart away complete.
My face turned pale as deadly pale,
    My legs refused to walk away,
And when she looked, what could I ail?
    My life and all seemed turned to clay.

And then my blood rushed to my face
    And took my eyesight quite away,
The trees and bushes round the place
    Seemed midnight at noonday.
I could not see a single thing,
    Words from my eyes did start –
They spoke as chords do from the string,
    And blood burnt round my heart.

Are flowers the winter's choice?
    Is love's bed always snow?
She seemed to hear my silent voice,
    Not love's appeals to know.

First Love

I never saw so sweet a face
    As that I stood before.
My heart has left its dwelling-place
    And can return no more.

John Clare (1820)

97

I Wish I Could Remember That First Day

I wish I could remember, that first day,
    First hour, first moment of your meeting me,
    If bright or dim the season, it might be
Summer or Winter for aught I can say;
So unrecorded did it slip away,
    So blind was I to see and to foresee,
    So dull to mark the budding of my tree
That would not blossom yet for many a May.
If only I could recollect it, such
    A day of days! I let it come and go
    As traceless as a thaw of bygone snow;
It seemed to mean so little, meant so much;
If only now I could recall that touch,
    First touch of hand in hand – Did one but know!

Christina Rossetti (1881)

Never the Time and the Place

Never the time and the place
    And the loved one all together!
This path – how soft to pace!
    This May – what magic weather!
Where is the loved one's face?
In a dream that loved one's face meets mine,
    But the house is narrow, the place is bleak
Where, outside, rain and wind combine
    With a furtive ear, if I strive to speak,
    With a hostile eye at my flushing cheek,
With a malice that marks each word, each sign!
O enemy sly and serpentine,
    Uncoil thee from the waking man!
        Do I hold the Past
        Thus firm and fast
Yet doubt if the Future hold I can?
This path so soft to pace shall lead
Thro' the magic of May to herself indeed!
Or narrow if needs the house must be,
Outside are the storms and strangers: we –
Oh, close, safe, warm sleep I and she,
 – I and she!

Robert Browning (1883)

The Sorrow of Love

The quarrel of the sparrows in the eaves,
    The full round moon and the star-laden sky,
And the loud song of the ever-singing leaves
    Had hid away earth's old and weary cry.

And then you came with those red mournful lips,
    And with you came the whole of the world's tears,
And all the sorrows of her labouring ships,
    And all burden of her myriad years.

And now the sparrows warring in the eaves,
    The crumbling moon, the white stars in the sky,
And the loud chanting of the unquiet leaves,
    Are shaken with earth's old and weary cry.

William Butler Yeats (1892)

100

My Heart Shall Be Thy Garden

My heart shall be thy garden. Come, my own,
    Into thy garden; thine be happy hours
    Among my fairest thoughts, my tallest flowers,
From root to crowning petal, thine alone.

Thine is the place from where the seeds are sown
    Up to the sky enclosed, with all its showers.
    But ah, the birds, the birds! Who shall build bowers
To keep these thine? O friend, the birds have flown.

For as these come and go, and quit our pine
    To follow the sweet season, or, new-comers,
      Sing one song only from our alder-trees.

My heart has thoughts, which, though thine eyes hold mine,
    Flit to the silent world and other summers,
      With wings that dip beyond the silver seas.

                        Alice Meynell (1896)

101

The Gardener (3)

In the morning I cast my net into the sea.

I dragged up from the dark abyss things of strange aspect and strange beauty – some shone like a smile, some glistened like tears, and some were flushed like the cheeks of a bride.

When with the day's burden I went home, my love was sitting in the garden idly tearing the leaves of a flower.

I hesitated for a moment, and then placed at her feet all that I had dragged up, and stood silent.

She glanced at them and said, 'What strange things are these? I know not of what use they are!'

I bowed my head in shame and thought, 'I have not fought for these, I did not buy them in the market; they are not fit gifts for her.'

Then the whole night through I flung them one by one into the street.

In the morning travellers came; they picked them up and carried them into far countries.

Rabindranath Tagore; (translated by the author 1913)

102

Lover's Return

Ma old time daddy
Came back home last night.
His face was pale an'
His eyes didn't look just right.

He says to me, 'I'm
Comin' home to you –
So sick an' lonesome
I don't know what to do.'

> *Oh, men treats women*
> *Just like a pair o' shoes.*
> *You men treats women*
> *Like a pair o' shoes –*
> *You kicks 'em round an'*
> *Does 'em like you choose.*

I looked at ma daddy –
Lawd! an' I wanted to cry.
He looked so thin –

102   Lover's Return

         Lawd! that I wanted to cry.
         But de devil told me:
             Damn a lover
             Comes home to die!

                               Langston Hughes (1931)

103

The Poet Speaks to His Love on the Telephone

In its sweet housing of wood
your voice watered the sand-dune of my heart.
To the south of my feet it was Spring,
north of my brow bracken in flower.

Down tight space a pine tree of light
sang without dawn or seedbed.
and for the first time my lament
strung crowns of hope across the roof.

Sweet distant voice poured for me.
Sweet distant voice savoured by me.
Sweet distant voice, dying away.

Distant as a dark wounded doe.
Sweet as a sob in snow.
Sweet and distant, in the very marrow!

Federico García Lorca (1935); Martin Sorrell (translated 2007)

104

Sea Canes

Half my friends are dead.
I will make you new ones, said earth.
No, give me them back, as they were, instead,
with faults and all, I cried.

Tonight I can snatch their talk
from the faint surf's drone
through the canes, but I cannot walk

on the moonlit leaves of ocean
down that white road alone,
or float with the dreaming motion

of owls leaving earth's load.
O earth, the number of friends you keep
exceeds those left to be loved.

The sea canes by the cliff flash green and silver;
they were the seraph lances of my faith,
but out of what is lost grows something stronger

that has the rational radiance of stone,
enduring moonlight, further than despair,
strong as the wind, that through dividing canes

brings those we love before us, as they were,
with faults and all, not nobler, just there.

           Derek Walcott (1976)

'The Poppy Signals Time to Scythe the Wheat'

I quote my mother though I don't suppose
she scanned it quite like that but found a brief
and simpler way to say that poppy grows
when wheat is ripe, like anger, love or grief.
For anger cannot foster change when dumb
to fault a man, nor love that cannot scythe
his pride fulfil him; grief will not succumb
to guilt that bears a grudge to bear a wreath.
No anger, love or grief will harvest good
till men can learn to listen, women learn
to speak, and turn their dreams to likelihood
of change and peace, redress and union.
    The day he died my mother cried all night,
    her tendrils round me, wound towards the light.

Mimi Khalvati (1990)

106

Temporary Sanity

What song now, scarecrow
Between the wind and I?
The sun will set my love will die
The seed plucked by indifferent beaks;
And to distant battle my foot hurries
My heart races faster than military drums.
Of kitchen and table and bed am I bereft
Willingly so and have hung my boots on twilight's nail.

The sun has not set my love has not died
The land is green my hand is around her heart
Tightening into a fist –

No, I am not drunk. My world from horizon to
Horizon has shrunk to a pinhead
Since I set eyes on her
Yesterday at three minutes to three.

Dambudzo Marechera (1992)

Transit

Urgencies of language: check-in, stand-by, take-off.
Everything apace, businesslike. But I'm happy here
Gazing at all the meetings and farewells. I love
To see those strangers' faces quickened and bare.
A lost arrival is wandering. A moment on edge,
He pans a lounge for his countersign of welcome.
A flash of greeting, sudden lightening of baggage,
As though he journeyed out only to journey home.
I watch a parting couple in their embrace and freeing.
The woman turns, a Veronica with her handkerchief
Absorbing into herself a last stain of a countenance.
She dissolves in crowds. An aura of her leaving glance
Travels through the yearning air. Tell me we live
For those faces wiped into the folds of our being.

Micheal O'Siadhail (1995)

108

Words Between Us

Language breaks down and sounds have no meaning.
Words splutter, dialogues die in mid air;
you and I cross and there is no meeting.

Eyes do not glance, there is no encounter,
postures are hidden and gestures are bare;
language breaks down and sounds have no meaning.

Even masques expose the fading actor,
curtains are drawn but invite no fanfare.
You and I cross and there is no meeting.

We are less than strangers in theatre,
playing separate parts in solitaire.
Language breaks down and sounds have no meaning.

Silence replays the role of the jester.
No more are we one, no longer a pair.
You and I cross and there is no meeting.

108 Words Between Us

Too many scenes have started to fester,

too many pauses are mimes that ensnare.

Language breaks down and sounds have no meaning.

You and I cross and there is no meeting.

Debjani Chatterjee (1997)

109

Song

to the iron-board's unconsidered flatness, praise
the necessity of clean, well-pressed cotton,
linen, denim, rayon – all fabrics, praise
the vexed countenance of a wrinkled white blouse,

blessed the conscience unable to reject,
in the heat of Monday morning lateness, the homily
preached in any language of a mother's strict
faith in the dogma of a properly ironed blouse,

praise the perfection of well-aligned pleats, razor-
sharp seams, wafer-neat collars and gabardine without a sheen,
praise the uncountable hours over boards that bear
the sizzling cuss-outs of steaming irons,

praise the only crossed legs allowed in her house
that stood the years' heavy-handed mission to
stamp stubborn creases out, praise
the spondaic call to level the terrain of a washed blouse,

109   Song

all praise the iron-board's appearance each Saturday evening
in the kitchen, chapel of my childhood
where I learnt to meditate the rosary of rhythm, scanning
the lines of her gliding, pressing, thumping hand

that sometimes softly sang, praise
the ever-rising incense of starch and steam,
praise the iron-board's wounded face and its sense
to share memories like a page, without shame,

praise the use-discoloured cover of slow
fading flowers – all praise the unremembered garden
of labour and to the white cotton blouse that now holds me
to the discipline of defying creases, shaping order,

praise the eternal surface that summons a mother,
praise her homely art whose first concern is form,
praise her days spent over convent blouses for a daughter
who never mastered her hand's command of an iron

praise be the iron-board, tapered at end
as if to ride the unruly surf, or
to make the markings of a pen

                                                      Jennifer Rahim (1999)

The Sculpture

From the mist's dense cape
I carve your body's shape –
gently sculpting, all morning.

With my eyes shut, I sit
amid the fog's heavy sheets
as its frost settles
on my cheek, ear, and nose.
The same hands,
the same lips, the same eyes –
I find them with such ease –
Your torso floats on that river;
I shall conquer its flow.
Your figure blossoms, freeing itself,
leaving behind sun's light
and fog's ephemeral body.
You're entwined with my soul –
its root, plinth, and depth.

Aminur Rahman (2001); Sudeep Sen (translated 2008)

111

A Feather

for Sepideh

Just as my dream
hears the sound of your steps,
that's when you enter
quietly, quietly on tiptoe.

You crawl under the sheet
like a kitten, your eyes
drinking me in.
Asleep or awake,
you lap the silk of my dreams.

In the moment it takes
to put your arms around my neck,
you're fast asleep on the pillow.

And I, half-asleep, half-awake,
just when I am drained of dreams,
am filled with you and replenished.

Shakila Azizzada (2004); Zuzanna Olszewska (translated 2012)

112

Poet, Lover, Birdwatcher

To force the pace and never to be still
Is not the way of those who study birds
Or women. The best poets wait for words.
The hunt is not an exercise of will
But patient love relaxing on a hill
To note the movement of a timid wing;
Until the one who knows that she is loved
No longer waits but risks surrendering –
In this the poet finds his moral proved,
Who never spoke before his spirit moved.

The slow movement seems, somehow, to say much more.
To watch the rarer birds, you have to go
Along deserted lanes and where the rivers flow
In silence near the source, or by a shore
Remote and thorny like the heart's dark floor.
And there the women slowly turn around,
Not only flesh and bone but myths of light
With darkness at the core, and sense is found
By poets lost in crooked, restless flight,
The deaf can hear, the blind recover sight.

Nissim Ezekiel (2005)

113

Arguments Left

A whole afternoon on a section of lawn near Invalides
Where men danced awkward dances with large kites
Strapped to their waists, and bright Frisbees tossed to
Levitating dogs as lovers embraced around picnic baskets.

We lay in the sun, bottle of wine, cheeses and baguette –
Still brandishing our silences, yet holding hands as if to say,
All this at some point will pass. And the blue sky held its blue,
The men with kites still danced their awkward dances –

Swaying and swinging, heeled into the lawn by the wind;
The colourful triangles weaving quiet flight into our view.
We fell asleep, then woke in the warm twilight – where
Shapes stood stencilled in the distance, but still not a word.

As we walked back to the apartment, over Alexandre bridge,
The city lights were lit. And there, in the evening heat
We stood overlooking the Seine by a lamppost with cupids
And garlands – our stubborn silence tightening our hands.

Togara Muzanenhamo (2006)

In the Chill

I wore no coat. My legs were bare.
I would not feel or see
The greyer nights, the cooler air.
Now it blows into me,

This autumn you concealed so well.
You told me it was spring
And made the swish of leaves that fell
Sound like awakening.

I was the fool in shorts and shades
Cloud-bathing in the chill.
I had been warned that summer fades
But spring meant I could still

Hope for the heat and light to start.
You were my longest day.
Your ice preserves my summer heart
Now winter's on the way.

Sophie Hannah (2007)

Gloves

Great-Grandmother's gloves were kept for funerals,
in tissue paper, limp as something stillborn.

She drew them on slowly, the grey silk
of the other self she wore.

Through each service they lay folded
on her lap, water-stained wings of a moth.

Afterwards, she gives them to me
to put away, still warm, and marked
where her wedding band has worn to gold wire.

She slides the long pins out of her hair,
and I brush until it hangs, a fall
of frozen water down her spine.

She sends me to the garden for fresh flowers
and sits for a while, just visible through the open door,
straight-backed and still, with naked hands.

Joanna Preston (2007)

116

Fast Forward

Holding the photograph of Mary Ellen,
my great-grandmother the midwife,
to gaze more closely at her face,
I see on my desk behind the frame
another picture, in another frame:
my blonde granddaughter holding her baby.
They are standing in a doorway,
just off to a lecture on *Beowulf*.

Suddenly a rushing of wings
as the generations between accelerate
like a fan of pages riffling over
or like the frames that rattled past
as I swooped into the anaesthetic
for my tonsillectomy, when I was nine.
Face after face, all with our imprint,
humming forwards. We can do anything.

Fleur Adcock (2010)

117

You May Have Heard of Me

My father was a bear.
He carried me through forest, sky
and over frozen sea. At night
I lay along his back
wrapped in fur and heat
and while I slept, he ran,
never stopping to rest, never
letting me fall.
He showed me how to be careful as stone
sharp as thorn and quick
as weather. When he hunted alone
he'd leave me somewhere safe – high up a tree
or deep within a cave.
And then a day went on …
He didn't come.
I looked and looked for him.
The seasons changed and changed again.
Sleep became my friend. It even brought my father back.
The dark was like his fur,
the sea's breathing echoed his breathing.
I left home behind, an empty skin.
Alone, I walked taller, balanced better.

So I came to the gates of this city
– tall, black gates with teeth.
Here you find me, keeping my mouth small,
hiding pointed teeth and telling stories,
concealing their truth as I conceal
the thick black fur on my back.

Shazea Quraishi (2015)

118

Netezon Laundrette

My mother cries while doing the washing.

This is the perfect moment for mothers to cry
because a revolving washing-machine drum
generally makes a racket.
I do hear her sobs, but they are so soft
they could be background noise.

A washing machine licks the day's wounds.
You can stuff in everything that doesn't fit in your head.
Sheets that haven't been slept on, for instance.
Or the tobacco smell in your cancer-patient grandfather's coat.
Long programme, sixty degrees, cleansing ritual.

For a long time I thought it wasn't fair that I had a mother who cried.
As if I had to go to school with a heavier bag
and singing Ring a Ring o' Roses I always thought
the tissue must be for my mother.

I explained the phenomenon of 'the crying mother' from the suspicion
that there wasn't enough water and that was why she stared into the machine
and thought long and hard about dead kittens, until
she could do the washing with her tears.

I grew up with salt rings in my clothes.

        Charlotte Van den Broeck (2015); David Colmer (translated 2020)

119

Beloved

Like a bedridden patient
unable to venture
beyond mattress and pillow,
forbidden anything but a visitor,

I burn inside.
I can't imbibe water.
I can't eat bread.
My lips have been sealed shut.

Many days I've bestowed
on battling with what's best,
no page has been unturned
in a bid to find my fate.

Beyond, others slumber soundly
in the night's blackness
but I engage in barren arguments,
bicker with each day's events.

I find best wishes tasteless.
I can't be pleased by social niceties.
I feel so phobic,
I like loneliness better,
ambling aimlessly through plains.

My heart belongs to him.
His love has beaten me.
I am under such bewitchment
I blanch at social gatherings,
I hold myself back.

My bearing and discretion,
all that's visible and audible
has been blunted
as I beseech in the wilderness.

I walk the brutal stony land,
bear the burning heat of sand
and ramble about
under the blasting sun
blind to my destination.

Many times I've been lost
and fallen into an abyss
risked my life in this bid,
got into bad situations.

All the winged birds,
brute animals, game animals,
the blond-coloured lion,

the blotched leopard,

the wider kin of wild beasts,

I settle with them in the open land and the bush.

The blows that I suffer,

the blues that hang over me,

the withering body

would be long gone

O Beloved, with the sight of you.

I observe my thirst,

my heart not functioning as before,

my lips benumbed,

my eyes blinking.

You're admired by men,

a brave hero.

Be my new moon –

unbreakable metal,

the desire of my being,

the best of all souls.

What comfort it would be

to hear that bright news.

Such balm to welcome you,

to abate the anxiety –

to behold you.

When, Beloved, will that be?

Asha Lul Mohamud Yusuf (2017); Clare Pollard (translated 2017)

120

Ode to a Pot Noodle

Salt-sharp, *umami*-hint of steam
seeps from the unfastened lid.

A cluster of noodles softens in a pot,
a body unstiffens in its new climate.

You sustain me during break, a breath
before an emergency bell tears a wall.

Oh, I will pedestal you on the counter
in the limelight of this lonely bulb,

this fast-paced night, this instant life.
A radiator click-clacks at the corner

where I find a vapour of my grandfather in his
arthritic dance, stirring something at the stove.

Garlics are chopped, peppercorns are cracked,
and the shadows of my *pamilya* ripple at the *mesa*.

120   Ode to a Pot Noodle

    I smile at their unflavoured conversations,
    how they slurp marrow from shanks of *bulalô* bones,

    spoon-scrape the meat from the carapaces of crabs.
    How everyone evaporates when the kettle snaps.

    And yes, this should have been an ode to you.
    Forgive me, forgive me.

Romalyn Ante (2020)

PART 5

Self

121

I Am As I Am

I am as I am and so will I be
But how that I am none knoweth truly.
Be it evil, be it well, be I bound, be I free,
I am as I am and so will I be.

I lead my life indifferently,
I mean no thing but honestly.
And though folks judge full diversely
I am as I am and so will I die.

I do not rejoice nor yet complain.
Both mirth and sadness I do refrain
And use the mean since folks will feign.
Yet I am as I am, be it pleasure or pain.

Diverse do judge as they do trow,
Some of pleasure and some of woe.
Yet for all that, nothing they know.
But I am as I am wheresoever I go.

But since that judgers do thus decay
Let every man his judgement say.
I will it take in sport and play
For I am as I am whosoever say nay.

Who judgeth well, well God him send.
Who judgeth evil, God them amend.
To judge the best therefore intend
For I am as I am and so will I end.

Yet some there be that take delight
To judge folks' thought for envy and spite.
But whether they judge me wrong or right
I am as I am and so do I write,

Praying you all that this do read
To trust it as you do your creed
And not to think I change my weed
For I am as I am however I speed.

But how that is I leave to you.
Judge as ye list, false or true.
Ye know no more than afore ye knew.
Yet I am as I am whatever ensue.

And from this mind I will not flee,
But to you all that misjudge me
I do protest, as ye may see,
That I am as I am and so will I be.

Thomas Wyatt (1557)

122

My Mind to Me a Kingdom Is

My mind to me a kingdom is
    Such perfect joy therein I find,
That it excels all other bliss
That world affords or grows by kind.
    Though much I want which most would have,
    Yet still my mind forbids to crave.

No princely pomp, no wealthy store,
No force to win the victory,
No wily wit to salve a sore,
No shape to feed a loving eye;
    To none of these I yield as thrall,
    For why? my mind doth serve for all.

I see how plenty suffers oft,
And hasty climbers soon do fall;
I see that those which are aloft
Mishap doth threaten most of all;
    They get with toil, they keep with fear;
    Such cares my mind could never bear.

Content I live, this is my stay,
I seek no more than may suffice,
I press to bear no haughty sway;
Look, what I lack my mind supplies.
    Lo, thus I triumph like a king,
      Content with that my mind doth bring.

Some have too much, yet still do crave,
I little have, and seek no more:
They are but poor, though much they have,
And I am rich with little store:
    They poor, I rich; they beg, I give;
      They lack, I leave; they pine, I live.

I laugh not at another's loss,
I grudge not at another's gain;
No worldly waves my mind can toss,
My state at one doth still remain.
    I fear no foe, I fawn no friend;
      I loathe not life, nor dread no end.

Some weigh their pleasure by their lust,
Their wisdom by their rage of will;
Their treasure is their only trust,
A cloaked craft their store of skill:
    But all the pleasure that I find
      Is to maintain a quiet mind.

122 My Mind to Me a Kingdom Is

My wealth is health and perfect ease,
My conscience clear my chief defence;
I neither seek by bribes to please,
Nor by desert to breed offence.
   Thus do I live, thus will I die;
   Would all did so, as well as I.

Edward Dyer (1588)

123

Now Leave and Let Me Rest

Now leave and let me rest. Dame Pleasure, be content –
Go choose among the best; my doting days be spent.
By sundry signs I see thy proffers are but vain,
And wisdom warneth me that pleasure asketh pain;
And Nature that doth know how time her steps doth try,
Gives place to painful woe, and bids me learn to die.

Since all fair earthly things, soon ripe, will soon be rot
And all that pleasant springs, soon withered, soon forgot,
And youth that yields men joys that wanton lust desires
In age repents the toys that reckless youth requires.
All which delights I leave to such as folly trains
By pleasures to deceive, till they do feel the pains.

And from vain pleasures past I fly, and fain would know
The happy life at last whereto I hope to go.
For words or wise reports ne yet examples gone
'Gan bridle youthful sports, till age came stealing on.
The pleasant courtly games that I do pleasure in,
My elder years now shames such folly to begin.

123   Now Leave and Let Me Rest

And all the fancies strange that fond delight brought forth
I do intend to change, and count them nothing worth.
For I by proffers vain am taught to know the skill
What might have been forborne in my young reckless will;
By which good proof I fleet from will to wit again,
In hope to set my feet in surety to remain.

Queen Elizabeth I (1589)

124

Sonnet 91

Some glory in their birth, some in their skill,
Some in their wealth, some in their body's force;
Some in their garments, though new-fangled ill;
Some in their hawks and hounds, some in their horse;
And every humour hath his adjunct pleasure,
Wherein it finds a joy above the rest;
But these particulars are not my measure:
All these I better in one general best.
Thy love is better than high birth to me,
Richer than wealth, prouder than garments' cost,
Of more delight than hawks and horses be;
And, having thee, of all men's pride I boast –
Wretched in this alone, that thou mayst take
All this away, and me most wretched make.

William Shakespeare (1609)

Sonnet 7

How soon hath time the subtle thief of youth,
    Stol'n on his wing my three and twentieth year!
    My hasting days fly on with full career,
    But my late spring no bud or blossom sheweth.
Perhaps my semblance might deceive the truth,
    That I to manhood am arrived so near,
    And inward ripeness doth much less appear,
    That some more timely-happy spirits endueth.
Yet be it less or more, or soon or slow,
    It shall be still in strictest measure even,
    To that same lot, however mean or high,
Toward which time leads me, and the will of heaven;
    All is, if I have grace to use it so,
    As ever in my great task-master's eye.

John Milton (1632)

126

from *Essay on Happiness*

[...] who are happy, 'twill be hard to say,
Since undisturbed it seldom lasts a day:
For who in smiles beholds the morning sun,
May weep before his short-lived journey's done.
All pleasures satiate and all objects cloy,
We crave, we grasp, but loathe the tasted joy:
Nor wealth nor beauty, friend's nor fortune's smile,
Can bless our moments, though they may beguile:
Nor wit with happiness can often grow,
A helpless friend, if not an arrant foe.

Where then? O where shall happiness be found?
Say, shall we search the rolling world around,
On borrowed pinions travel through the sky,
Or to the centre drive our piercing eye?
Cease, busy fool: is happiness thy care?
Pierce thy own breast, and thou wilt find it there:
Drive thence the passions, and the guilt expel,
And call fair Virtue to the polished cell.

126   from Essay on Happiness

      Call soft Content with all her smiling train;
      Peace for thy health, and Patience for thy pain:
      Then not till then, O Man, thy heart shall know
      Bliss so adored, but seldom found below.

Mary Leapor (1748)

127

from *The Happy Solitude*

Fatigu'd with life, I yet methinks would live,
Free'd from the pains that fraud or folly give;
Where'er I turn, where'er direct my flight,
Folly, continual folly, meets my sight;
Man, thoughtless man, to sacred reason blind,
Obeys the dictates of his restless mind,
Ambition, vengeance, avarice conspire,
With luxury's delights, and anger's fire.
One toils for opulence, and one for fame,
To leave a fortune, or to leave a name;
Each labours restless for mistaken bliss,
All the plain road of true contentment miss;
With reason's scorn, with dignity's disgrace,
There fools contend, to fill the highest place;
There they like vapours, when exhal'd too high,
Shine glaring meteors of this lower sky;
There for a while, all dazzling they amaze,
And fright the world with their portentous blaze;
Till, having wasted all their boasted light,
They sink unpity'd to the realms of night.

127   from The Happy Solitude

    For me, contented with an humble state,
'Twas ne'er my care, or fortune, to be great;
No pomp, no grandeur, no desire of fame,
No sordid wealth was ever yet my aim;
My highest wish, a well instructed mind,
Content with little, and to heav'n resign'd;
No passion but the noblest fill'd my breast,
And all I sought, and all I seek is rest,
Free from tumult'ous cares and busy strife,
May I enjoy the harmless sweets of life;
In rural shades, like the first fam'd abodes
Of happy men, oft visited by Gods,
There the remains of ling'ring life employ,
In holy solitude and silent joy,
No busy cares, should there my soul molest,
No past unkindness discompose my breast,
My still retreat, so pleasant, yet so low,
That all would envy, but that none should know;
Joy, peace, and love, with me should ever reign,
And true religion grace the godlike train;
There pleas'd and calm I'd look with pity down,
On those who bear th' incumb'rance of a crown.
Then, O great Arbiter of all below,
A ray of wisdom on my soul bestow,
That I may wisely Nature's works explore,
And thro' her works, may Nature's God adore;
Then with devotion fir'd I'd still address
My songs to thee, thy Providence to bless;

from The Happy Solitude

Thus calmly would my soul thy will await,
Nor wish a long, nor fear a shorter date;
But when death calls I'd meet him as a friend;
Thus would I live, and thus my life should end.

Anna Williams (1766)

128

On Virtue

    O Thou bright jewel in my aim I strive
To comprehend thee. Thine own words declare
Wisdom is higher than a fool can reach.
I cease to wonder, and no more attempt
Thine height t'explore, or fathom thy profound.
But, O my soul, sink not into despair,
Virtue is near thee, and with gentle hand
Would now embrace thee, hovers o'er thine head.
Fain would the heav'n-born soul with her converse,
Then seek, then court her for her promis'd bliss.

    Auspicious queen, thine heav'nly pinions spread,
And lead celestial *Chastity* along;
Lo! now her sacred retinue descends,
Array'd in glory from the orbs above.
Attend me, *Virtue*, thro' my youthful years!
O leave me not to the false joys of time!
But guide my steps to endless life and bliss.
Greatness, or *Goodness*, say what I shall call thee,
To give an higher appellation still,
Teach me a better strain, a nobler lay,
O Thou, enthron'd with Cherubs in the realms of day!

                                               Phillis Wheatley (1773)

129

Dedication (from *Faust*)

Uncertain shapes, visitors from the past
At whom I darkly gazed so long ago,
My heart's mad fleeting visions – now at last
Shall I embrace you, must I let you go?
Again you haunt me: come then, hold me fast!
Out of the mist and murk you rise, who so
Besiege me, and with magic breath restore,
Stirring my soul, lost youth to me once more.

You bring back memories of happier days
And many a well-loved ghost again I greet;
As when some old half-faded legend plays
About our ears, sorrowing strains repeat
My journey through life's labyrinthine maze,
Old griefs revive, old friends, old loves I meet,
Those dear companions, by their fate's unkind
Decree cut short, who left me here behind.

They cannot hear my present music, those
Few souls who listened to my early song;
They are far from me now who were so close,
And their first answering echo has so long

129   Dedication (from Faust)

Been silent. My lament is heard, who knows
By whom? I shudder as the nameless throng
Applauds it. Are they living still, those friends
Whom once it moved, scattered to the world's ends?

And I am seized by long unwonted yearning
For that still, solemn spirit-realm which then
Was mine; its hovering lisping tones returning
Sigh as from some Aeolian harp, as when
I sang them first; I tremble, and my burning
Tears flow, my stern heart melts to love again.
All that I now possess seems far away
And vanished worlds are real to me today.

   Johann Wolfgang von Goethe (1808); David Luke (translated 2005)

130

from *Lara, a Tale*

XVIII

There was in him a vital scorn of all:
As if the worst had fallen which could befall,
He stood a stranger in this breathing world,
An erring Spirit from another hurled;
A thing of dark imaginings, that shaped
By choice the perils he by chance escaped;
But 'scaped in vain, for in their memory yet
His mind would half exult and half regret:
With more capacity for love than Earth
Bestows on most of mortal mould and birth.
His early dreams of good outstripped the truth,
And troubled Manhood followed baffled Youth;
With thought of years in phantom chase misspent,
And wasted powers for better purpose lent;
And fiery passions that had poured their wrath
In hurried desolation o'er his path,
And left the better feelings all at strife
In wild reflection o'er his stormy life;
But haughty still, and loth himself to blame,
He called on Nature's self to share the shame,
And charged all faults upon the fleshly form
She gave to clog the soul, and feast the worm;

130 from Lara, a Tale

Till he at last confounded good and ill,
And half mistook for fate the acts of will:
Too high for common selfishness, he could
At times resign his own for others' good,
But not in pity – not because he ought,
But in some strange perversity of thought,
That swayed him onward with a secret pride
To do what few or none would do beside;
And this same impulse would, in tempting time,
Mislead his spirit equally to crime;
So much he soared beyond, or sunk beneath,
The men with whom he felt condemned to breathe,
And longed by good or ill to separate
Himself from all who shared his mortal state;
His mind abhorring this had fixed her throne
Far from the world, in regions of her own:
Thus coldly passing all that passed below,
His blood in temperate seeming now would flow:
Ah! happier if it ne'er with guilt had glowed,
But ever in that icy smoothness flowed!
'Tis true, with other men their path he walked,
And like the rest in seeming did and talked,
Nor outraged Reason's rules by flaw nor start,
His Madness was not of the head, but heart;
And rarely wandered in his speech, or drew
His thoughts so forth as to offend the view.

George Gordon, Lord Byron (1814)

131

Thoughts on My Sick-Bed

And has the remnant of my life
Been pilfered of this sunny Spring?
And have its own prelusive sounds
Touched in my heart no echoing string?

Ah! say not so – the hidden life
Couchant within this feeble frame
Hath been enriched by kindred gifts,
That, undesired, unsought-for, came.

With joyful heart in youthful days
When fresh each season in its Round
I welcomed the earliest Celandine
Glittering upon the mossy ground;

With busy eyes I pierced the lane
In quest of known and *un*known things,
 – The primrose a lamp on its fortress rock,
The silent butterfly spreading its wings,

Thoughts on My Sick-Bed

The violet betrayed by its noiseless breath,
The Daffodil dancing in the breeze,
The carolling thrush, on his naked perch,
Towering above the budding trees.

Our cottage-hearth no longer our home,
Companions of Nature were we,
The Stirring, the Still, the Loquacious, the Mute –
To all we gave our sympathy.

Yet never in those careless days
When spring-time in rock, field, or bower
Was but a fountain of earthly hope,
A promise of fruits & the *splendid* flower,

No – then I never felt a bliss
That might with *that* compare
Which, piercing to my couch of rest
Came on the vernal air,

When loving Friends an offering brought,
The first flowers of the year,
Culled from the precincts of our home,
From nooks to Memory dear.

With some sad thoughts the work was done,
Unprompted and unbidden,
But joy it brought to my *hidden* life,
To consciousness no longer hidden.

I felt a Power unfelt before,
Controlling weakness, languor, pain;
It bore me to the Terrace walk
I trod the Hills again; –

No prisoner in this lonely room,
I *saw* the green Banks of the Wye,
Recalling thy prophetic words,
Bard, Brother, Friend from infancy!

No need of motion, or of strength,
Or even the breathing air:
 – I thought of Nature's loveliest scenes;
And with Memory I was there.

                              Dorothy Wordsworth (1832)

132

Long Time a Child

Long time a child, and still a child, when years
Had painted manhood on my cheek, was I, –
For yet I lived like one not born to die;
A thriftless prodigal of smiles and tears,
No hope I needed, and I knew no fears.
But sleep, though sweet, is only sleep, and waking,
I waked to sleep no more, at once o'ertaking
The vanguard of my age, with all arrears
Of duty on my back. Nor child, nor man,
Nor youth, nor sage, I find my head is grey,
For I have lost the race I never ran:
A rathe December blights my lagging May;
And still I am a child, though I be old:
Time is my debtor for my years untold.

Hartley Coleridge (1833)

Stanzas: 'Often rebuked, yet always back returning'

Often rebuked, yet always back returning
    To those first feelings that were born with me,
And leaving busy chase of wealth and learning
    For idle dreams of things which cannot be;

To-day, I will seek not the shadowy region;
    Its unsustaining vastness waxes drear;
And visions rising, legion after legion,
    Bring the unreal world too strangely near.

I'll walk, but not in old heroic traces,
    And not in paths of high morality,
And not among the half-distinguished faces,
    The clouded forms of long-past history.

I'll walk where my own nature would be leading:
    It vexes me to choose another guide:
Where the grey flocks in ferny glens are feeding;
    Where the wild wind blows on the mountain side.

133 Stanzas: 'Often rebuked, yet always back returning'

What have those lonely mountains worth revealing?
More glory and more grief than I can tell:
The earth that wakes *one* human heart to feeling
Can centre both the worlds of Heaven and Hell.

Emily Brontë (1850)

134

from *My Heart and I*

I

Enough! we're tired, my heart and I.
    We sit beside the headstone thus,
    And wish that name were carved for us.
The moss reprints more tenderly
    The hard types of the mason's knife,
    As heaven's sweet life renews earth's life
With which we're tired, my heart and I.

II

You see we're tired, my heart and I.
    We dealt with books, we trusted men,
    And in our own blood drenched the pen,
As if such colours could not fly
    We walked too straight for fortune's end,
    We loved too true to keep a friend;
At last we're tired, my heart and I.

III

How tired we feel, my heart and I!
    We seem of no use in the world;
    Our fancies hang grey and uncurled
About men's eyes indifferently;
    Our voice which thrilled you so, will let
    You sleep; our tears are only wet:
What do we here, my heart and I?

Elizabeth Barrett Browning (1862)

What the Heart Is Like

Officially the heart
is oblong, muscular,
and filled with longing.

But anyone who has painted the heart knows
that it is also

spiked like a star
and sometimes bedraggled
like a stray dog at night
and sometimes powerful
like an archangel's drum.

And sometimes cube-shaped
like a draughtsman's dream
and sometimes gaily round
like a ball in a net.

And sometimes like a thin line
and sometimes like an explosion.

135   What the Heart Is Like

And in it is
only a river,
a weir
and at most one little fish
by no means golden.

More like a grey
jealous
loach.

It certainly isn't noticeable
at first sight.

Anyone who has painted the heart knows
that first he had to
discard his spectacles,
his mirror,
throw away his fine-point pencil
and carbon paper

and for a long while
walk
outside.

Miroslav Holub (1963); Ian Milner (translated 1987)

136

The Widower in the Country

I'll get up soon, and leave my bed unmade.
I'll go outside and split off kindling wood
from the yellow-box log that lies beside the gate,
and the sun will be high, for I get up late now.

I'll drive my axe in the log and come back in
with my armful of wood, and pause to look across
the Christmas paddocks aching in the heat,
the windless trees, the nettles in the yard …
and then I'll go in, boil water and make tea.

This afternoon, I'll stand out on the hill
and watch my house away below, and how
the roof reflects the sun and makes my eyes
water and close on bright webbed visions smeared
on the dark of my thoughts to dance and fade away.
Then the sun will move on, and I will simply watch,
or work, or sleep. And evening will come on.

136   The Widower in the Country

> Getting near dark, I'll go home, light the lamp
> and eat my corned-beef supper, sitting there
> at the head of the table. Then I'll go to bed.
> Last night I thought I dreamed – but when I woke
> the screaming was only a possum ski-ing down
> the iron roof on little moonlit claws.

Les Murray (1965)

from *Solitude*

I

Right here I was nearly killed one night in February.
My car slewed on the ice, sideways,
into the other lane. The oncoming cars –
their headlights – came nearer.

My name, my daughters, my job
slipped free and fell behind silently,
farther and farther back. I was anonymous,
like a schoolboy in a lot surrounded by enemies.

The approaching traffic had powerful lights.
They shone on me while I turned and turned
the wheel in a transparent fear that moved like eggwhite.
The seconds lengthened out – making more room –
they grew long as hospital buildings.

It felt as if you could just take it easy
and loaf a bit
before the smash came.

137   from Solitude

> Then firm land appeared: a helping sandgrain
> or a marvelous gust of wind. The car took hold
> and fish-tailed back across the road.
> A signpost shot up, snapped off – a ringing sound –
> tossed into the dark.
>
> Came all quiet. I sat there in my seatbelt
> and watched someone tramp through the blowing snow
> to see what had become of me.
>
> Tomas Tranströmer (1966); Robert Bly (translated 2001)

Two short poems from *Letters to Martha*

The companionship of bluegum trees

their sheen and spangle against the midday winter sun

and the companionable nudge of my heart

knocking against my mind and memory

with evocation of my student hazy days

condemns me once again

labels me poet dreamer troubadour

unreal unworldly muddle-headed fool

while the trees nod and swagger

and the level sunlight flows.

    8 *July* 1966

***

Steeling oneself to face the day

girding one's self for the wrap of clothes

bracing oneself for the thrust of the world

one buckles to buttons and zips and belts:

With the gritted reluctance and indifference to pain

with which one enters an unsought fight

one accepts the challenge the bullying day thrusts down.

Dennis Brutus (1968)

Epitaph

We are this union

of water salt and earth

of sunshine and flesh

bespattering the sun

no more among the sea marks

but because there is this song

which ruins all the gulfs

which recreates a genesis

of wind weather and flesh!

I predict a babel

of unoxidized steel

or of crossed blood

mixed in the dregs of all surges!

After the red man,

after the black man,

after the yellow man,

after the white man,

there is already the man of bronze

sole alloy of the soft fires

we have still to ford.

Tchicaya U Tam'si (1970); Gerald Moore (translated 1970)

140

You Won't Believe It

You won't believe it, I have stars in my fists.
When I squeeze them, patterns of light
seep out from every crevice,
and in my glass-like bones quicksilver glows green.
I have stars in my fists,
but I fear someone might steal them.
I stare at every corner.
I listen for every sound.
I see someone lurking in the dark:
a monster from the tales my nanny used to tell me,
his eyes volcanoes, spewing anger
like streams of violet and crimson lava.
It's him, I thought, the extortionist,
coveting in the darkness
the stars I hold so dear.

He attacked me. I screamed.
I realized, to win this fight I needed a weapon.
I threw at his head every rock I could get my hands on.
He fell, wounded, squirming in his own blood.

The monster has fallen from the heights to such dust.
But you won't believe it:
I have no more stars in my fists.

Simin Behbahani (1985); Farzaneh Milani and Kaveh Safa (translated 1992)

141

Mistress of My Own Being

Untied of all binding knots –
the tears and ties of time,
freed of haunting memories and regrets,
feelings of contentment rush on
like soft tidal waves,
till slowly, they envelop me.

Thinking of nothing,
wrapped up in my own warmth,
in scents and steam-blankets,
protected in my contentment,
I lie calm and supreme.

In this sweet sanctuary,
I have no need of food or man,
I feel no need for tomorrows,
no need for sound or voices,
only the soothing silence of the night.

141 Mistress of My Own Being

Through the dancing folds
of the lacy petticoat of the window,
I see the yellowness of the night;
a huge brilliant eye in heaven
probing me.

In amorous splendour,
she throws out hands full of golden arrows
reaching for the hidden apples
in the folds of my mind.

Not even the sensuality of the moon
can move me now in my calm
Peace and contentment,
let those be my virtue,
as I lie calm and supreme,
Mistress of my own being.

Ifi Amadiume (1986)

142

What I Learned in the Wars

What did I learn in the wars:
To march in time to the swinging of arms and legs
like a pump pumping an empty well;
To march in procession and to be alone in the fray;
To bury myself in pillows and covers and the body of my beloved,
and to shout "Mother," without her hearing,
and to shout "God," without believing in Him –
and even if I did believe in Him
I would never tell Him about war
the way we keep from children their parents' atrocities.

What else did I learn? I learned to keep open an escape route:
Abroad, I take a room in a hotel
near the airport or train station,
and even in halls of rejoicing
always look for the little door
with EXIT written over it in red letters.

Battle too begins
like rhythmic dance drums, and its end
is "withdrawal with the dawn." Forbidden love
and battle both, at times, conclude this way.

What I Learned in the Wars

But above all I learned the knowledge of camouflage,
so that I would not stand out, not be recognized,
so I would not be distinguishable from my surroundings,
even from my beloved,
so I would seem a bush, or a sheep,
a tree, a shadow of a tree,
a doubt, a shadow of a doubt,
an electrified fence, a dead stone,
a house, a cornerstone.

If I were a prophet I would dim the brilliance of vision
and black out my faith with black paper
and cover with netting my thoughts of divine chariots.

And when the time comes I'll put on the camouflage of my end:
the white of clouds and an expanse of sky blue
and endless stars.

                Yehuda Amichai (1988); Karen Alkalay-Gut (translated 1989)

143

Narcissus at the Flea Market

Thought I'd have a rummage, you never know.
One man's thrash is another man's treasure
and all that. Out of attics and sheds come objects
of desire, especially ones with surfaces that reflect
my own self-sparkling. That's why I have little time
for rugs and carpets. Fine for stepping on.
But they never return my radiant reflection.
The same goes for old books whose covers,
however classic, are no use for viewing one's image.
Might as well be staring into a brick.
But mirrors, ah mirrors, now you're talking my language.

Over the years I've seen myself in the oval,
in the round, scalloped, pebbled, full-length pedestalled,
down to my own handheld silvered darling.
Of course, I'd already done pools, puddles, lakes, rivers,
before graduating to mirrors and shop windows.
So imagine my joy, among a random galaxy of junk,
to encounter my familiar features in a bathroom tile,

Narcissus at the Flea Market

an art deco coffee table, not to mention forgotten vinyl.
I like to call it my flea market epiphany.
Now every time I gaze into those round black discs,
I see the planet of my face beckoning me to me.

John Agard (2013)

144

Bones

1

It runs in some families
this stiffening, in the early forties,

around the knee, the need
to invest more effort

in the flexion of thumb
and maybe the more attentive

hear a wind blowing
through the card palace

of their bones – a premonition
of the crumble

of resolve and calcium
and fortitude that some call

ageing. And so they pull in their limbs
like ancient drawbridges,

watch roaring desires sputter
into gentler static

though there were always other ways to get here.

2

When the heart's sludgy tributaries
grow dry,
trust the bones.

Their dry winter wisdom
will not deceive you

for in their white chalk quarry
lies something truer

than any of the fruity varieties of love
you have known.

One day the fingers will uncurl again,
the nostrils twitch, eyes widen

and the body will return to what it's always been –
    old antenna,

tuned promiscuously
springward.

But even then,
remember,
> try to remember

the bones.

Arundhathi Subramaniam (2014)

145

The Way I Am

You don't resent the sun for shining at noon;

It wouldn't be right to assume it's undermining the moon.

You don't resent the tide for climbing the land;

You understand that it's not undermining the sand.

You don't challenge the boundlessness of your mind span

You don't ask a penguin or an ostrich why it can't fly, but time can.

Your lungs can understand a breeze that breathes over trees and leaves

Whenever it decides to pass by the scene.

You don't ask the grass why it's green.

You don't question how fast life has been.

These things are as natural as the things that make a man.

So you can understand why I am the way I am.

George the Poet (2015)

146

Kindness

Before you know what kindness really is
you must lose things,
feel the future dissolve in a moment
like salt in a weakened broth.
What you held in your hand,
what you counted and carefully saved,
all this must go so you know
how desolate the landscape can be
between the regions of kindness.
How you ride and ride
thinking the bus will never stop,
the passengers eating maize and chicken
will stare out the window forever.

Before you learn the tender gravity of kindness,
you must travel where the Indian in a white poncho
lies dead by the side of the road.
You must see how this could be you,
how he too was someone
who journeyed through the night with plans
and the simple breath that kept him alive.

146 Kindness

Before you know kindness as the deepest thing inside,
you must know sorrow as the other deepest thing.
You must wake up with sorrow.
You must speak to it till your voice
catches the thread of all sorrows
and you see the size of the cloth.

Then it is only kindness that makes sense anymore,
only kindness that ties your shoes
and sends you out into the day to mail letters and purchase bread,
only kindness that raises its head
from the crowd of the world to say
It is I you have been looking for,
and then goes with you everywhere
like a shadow or a friend.

Naomi Shihab Nye (2015)

Kumukanda

Since I haven't danced among my fellow initiates,
following a looped procession from woods at the edge
of a village, Tata's people would think me unfinished –
a child who never sloughed off the childish estate
to cross the river boys of our tribe must cross
in order to die and come back grown.

I was raised in a strange land, by small increments:
when I bathed my mother the days she was too weak,
when auntie broke the news and I chose a yellow suit
and white shoes to dress my mother's body,
at the grave-side when the man I almost grew to call
dad, though we both needed a hug, shook my hand.

If my alternate self, who never left, could see me
what would he make of these literary pretensions,
this need to speak with a tongue that isn't mine?
Would he be strange to me as I to him, frowning
as he greets me in the language of my father
and my father's father and my father's father's father?

Kayo Chingonyi (2017)

Maracas Beach Prayer

With sandy grit, with salt and weeds
each large wave returns to beach.
Make my life this simple, Lord.

The waves consume you where you stand
and feet float up from shallow sand.
Make my life this simple, Lord.

I swim past their crash to gentle seas
and tread still water with my feet.
Make my life this simple, Lord.

Some men pull nets, their veins like streams,
and kids, they kick their ball and scream.
Make my life this simple, Lord.

Of all the gifts you have to give
if this could be a way to live,
make my life this simple, Lord.

Roger Robinson (2019)

149

The Day

will come like a breath when you refuse
any negotiations on your body, your eyes
stop being a lighthouse for compliments about

how good your English is, your smile can take
that weekend off, kick back and choose
any seat it likes. Your politeness will remain

in your pocket, no longer a passport,
and your skin will stop being an entry
on a colour chart that has no name for

the brow of a Himalayan sunrise or the shade
of rain on an egg-fried-rice afternoon, or the
powder of a bleeding temple. One day white

people won't skim this poem about your
body, they will have learned to listen to a
sea that isn't a tremulous roar of pebbles,

The Day

      to see some sky that isn't theirs, a river of litter
      running to a plastic beach, a difficult
      breeze, they will hear those vehicles rattling

      on an earthquake road, the laugh of a landscape,
      houses filled with monsoon green, flowers,
      dogs barking, the cries and laughter of a body

      that's mine

Mukahang Limbu (2023)

150

Picture of Girl and Small Boy (Burij, Gaza, 2014)

I would like to tell her not to wear such flimsy shoes,
that rubble contains the whole spectrum of knowable
and unknowable dangers: sheets of metal, ripped
to knife edge, live wires, bloated arms reaching

for light. Her hair, scraped back into a ponytail,
is open to sky; remnants of buildings filter down
one concrete chunk at a time, and the midday bells
of rockets ring out above her. She carries a boy

on her still narrow hips, his legs entwined around
her yellow dungarees. Like a rodeo rider, his left arm
grips her shoulder to steady himself, or her,
while his torso reels back and away; his body

is asking to slow down, to turn back. Instead,
her eyes comb the ground for a next step, fingers
of her free hand curled into a claw, as if
to frighten off what she somehow sees ahead.

Marjorie Lotfi (2023)

Index of First Lines

A Bird came down the Walk 21
A dream, a dream is it all – the season 128
A whole afternoon on a section of lawn near Invalides 202
Accept, my God, the Praises which I bring 6
Across the blackened pond and back again 147
afar, like a dawn in the midnight 126
After a black day, I play Haydn 142
All the squares of trampoline are taken 149
And has the remnant of my life 235
And in the frosty season, when the sun 125
And now at the end of the round 145
As I climb the slope with the sledge in tow 152
As if words were not enough 133
At last it lifts 163

Before you know what kindness really is 263
Blushed with blood and false summits, outcast 110
But hark! Distress with screaming Voice draws nigh'r 65

Clustered in a mallee ash, swinging upside down 40
Come live with me, and be my love 174

Dark house, by which once more I stand 69
Day and night endlessly you have flown effortless of wing 38
Descend ye Nine! descend and sing 116

Early in the spring 58
Enough! we're tired, my heart and I 241
Exert thy Voice, sweet Harbinger of Spring! 8

Farewell, thou child of my right hand, and joy 173
Fatigu'd with life, I yet methinks would live 227

Five forty-four am is not morning 104
From the mist's dense cape 199

Great-Grandmother's gloves were kept for funerals 204

Had we but World enough, and Time 176
Half my friends are dead 190
Hither thou com'st: the busy wind all night 3
Holding the photograph of Mary Ellen 205
Hour of dusk 24
How soon hath time the subtle thief of youth 224
How vainly men themselves amaze 62

I am as I am and so will I be 216
I have laid them 78
I heard a cough 50
I know this frosted landscape 97
I loafed about at leisure munching pears 138
I ne'er was struck before that hour 180
I quote my mother though I don't suppose 192
I saw red evening through the rain 70
I stoop to pick up my footprints 102
I think of a tiger. The fading light enhances 26
I want to remember the fallen palm 32
I was not born from your womb 76
I was the first of birds to sing 165
I wish I could remember, that first day 182
I wore no coat. My legs were bare 203
I would like to tell her not to wear such flimsy shoes 269
I'll get up soon, and leave my bed unmade 245
I've known exposed till, soft ground returning 101
If it could be done, would you want 44
Imagine him coming back from a war 91
In its sweet housing of wood 189
In the beginning of time 54
In the morning I cast my net into the sea 186
Is Paradise an island of perfection 108

It is 12:20 in New York a Friday 140
It runs in some families 259

Just as my dream 200
Just like as in a nest of boxes round 5
Just off the highway to Rochester, Minnesota 28

Language breaks down and sounds have no meaning 195
Left at the lodge and park, snout to America 154
Like a bedridden patient 210
Like a huge Python, winding round and round 72
Long time a child, and still a child, when years 238

Ma old time daddy 187
Maybe enough light 167
My aspens dear, whose airy cages quelled 19
My father was a bear 206
My heart aches, and a drowsy numbness pains 11
My heart shall be thy garden. Come, my own 185
My mind to me a kingdom is 218
My mother cries while doing the washing 208

Never the time and the place 183
No, helpless thing, I cannot harm thee now 15
Now leave and let me rest. Dame Pleasure, be content 221
Now see prepared to lead the sprightly dance 118

O joyous, blossoming, ever-blessed flowers! 2
O Thou bright jewel in my aim I strive 230
Officially the heart 243
Often rebuked, yet always back returning 239
Once I thought the land I had loved and known 75
Outside that house, I stood like a dog 80
Over the vast summer hills 82

Right here I was nearly killed one night in February 247
Rolled half onto its back 56

Salt-sharp, *umami*-hint of steam 213
Scanning the bars, his gaze is grown so numb 23
Seats of my youth, when every sport could please 67
See! with what constant Motion 114
She is away 159
Since I haven't danced among my fellow initiates 265
Small, viewless Æronaut, that by the line 10
Some glory in their birth, some in their skill 223
Song closed up the air 136
Stranger in his own element 30

That January, the sea brought us a message 48
The companionship of bluegum trees 249
The day will come when papers 52
The first thing to remember about flip turns 169
The kite, completed thus, is borne along 120
The late hour trickles to morning. The cattle low profusely by the anthill 151
The quarrel of the sparrows in the eaves 184
The vesper bells rang out the day 130
The world begins at a kitchen table. No matter what, we must eat to live 88
There was in him a vital scorn of all 233
They go down to the expressways, baskets 46
They hug their house around them 90
This is the only way for the mind 111
This is the spot where the walls stood 93
This level reach of blue is not my sea 73
This one is enormous: rough-cut 42
This poem is like a house where I once lived 109
This same evening that I write I witnessed 74
This time he fell in the abyss on his horse, and the Sun fell with him 95
Thou tiney loiterer on the barleys beard 17
Though the fall of an apple is not, like the fall 34
Thought I'd have a rummage, you never know 257
Through sunlight and shadow dust swirls 86
To force the pace and never to be still   201
to the iron-board's unconsidered flatness, praise 197

Uncertain shapes, visitors from the past 231
Untied of all binding knots 253
Urgencies of language: check-in, stand-by, take-off 194

Water of jellyfish 36
We are this union 250
We huddled on street corners 84
What did I learn in the wars 255
What song now, scarecrow 193
What walls and gables, wonders still of workmanship 99
when faces called flowers float out of the ground 135
When in the chronicle of wasted time 172
When my April showers me with kisses 157
When the returning sun begins to smile 122
who are happy, 'twill be hard to say 225
Why does this written doe bound through these written woods 143
Wife and servant are the same 178
will come like a breath when you refuse 267
With sandy grit, with salt and weeds 266
Without wheels their boy bodies are eloquent 155

Years back and full of echoes 161
You don't resent the sun for shining at noon 262
You will see them pacing platform tracks 106
You won't believe it, I have stars in my fists 251

Acknowledgements

The authors and publishers acknowledge the following sources of copyright material and are grateful for the permissions granted. While every effort has been made, it has not always been possible to identify the sources of all the material used, or to trace all copyright holders. If any omissions are brought to our notice, we will be happy to include the appropriate acknowledgements on reprinting.

'The Panther' by Rainer Maria Rilke, translated by Len Kriask in *New Poems*, Camden House, permission conveyed through Copyright Clearance Center, Inc; 'Autumn' by Melissanthi, translated by Kimon Friar in *Modern Greek Poetry*, Efstathiadis Group S A and Simon & Schuster; 'The Other Tiger' by Jorge Luis Borges, translated by Alastair Reid © 1999 by Maria Kodama, translation © 1999 by Alistair Reid from *Selected Poems* by Jorges Luis Borges, edited by Alexander Coleman. Used by permission of Viking Books, an imprint of Penguin Publishing Group, a division of Penguin Random House LLC US; 'A Blessing' from *Collected Poems* © 1971 by James Wright. Published by Wesleyan University Press. Used with permission; 'Oblivion' by Ellis Ayitey Komey in *Messages: Poems from Ghana* compiled by Kofi Awoonor and G.Adali Morrt, Heinemann; 'Suns and Straws' by Dorothy Donnelly, first published in *Kudzu and Other Poems* (©Dorothy Donnelly 1978), used by kind permission of the author's Estate; 'Water of Jellyfish' by Coral Bracho, translated from Spanish by Tom Boll with the poet Katherine Pierpoint. First published in *My Voice* by The Poetry Translation Centre and Bloodaxe Books, 2012; '*Toroa*: Albatross' by Hone Tuwhare, used by kind permission of the Estate of Hone Tuwhare; 'On the Random Distribution of King Parrots' by John Kinsella in *The Ascension of Sheep, Collected Poems Volume One (1980–2005)* used by permission of the University of Western Australia Publishing and David Godwin Associates for John Kinsella; 'The Camel Comes to Us from the Barbarians', from *On the Bus with Rosa Parks* by Rita Dove. Copyright © 1999 by Rita Dove. Used by permission of W W Norton & Company, Inc; 'Frog' by Marilene Phipps, Carcanet Publishers, England, *New Caribbean Poetry*, Anthology, Spring 2007; From 'Endless Inter-States': 1 by Sina Queryas from *Expressway*, Coach House Books, 2009, used by permission of the publisher; 'The Whale' by Katrina Porteous from *Two Countries* (Bloodaxe Books, 2015); 'Fox' by Alice Oswald from *Falling Awake: Poems* by Alice Oswald © 2016, Alice Oswald. Reprinted by permission of The Random House Group Limited and by permission of W W Norton & Company, Inc; '#ExtinctionRebellion' by Pascal Petit from *Tiger Girl* (Bloodaxe Books, 2020); 'Whale' by Cindy Botha originally published in the *Ginkgo Poetry Prize Ecopoetry Anthology* 2021, Poetry School, London, 2022; 'The Year of One Thousand Fires' by Andre Naffis-Sahely from *High Desert* (Bloodaxe Books, 2022); 'The Sun Wanders, Searching for Shade' by Alari, translated from Tamil by Shash Trevett. First published in *Adda Stories: Translations South and South-East Asia* (Issue 4: 2021). Reprinted in V Ravinthiran, S Seneviratne, S Trevett (eds.) *Out of Sri Lanka: Tamil, Sinhala and English Poetry from Sri Lanka and its Diasporas* (Bloodaxe Books, 2023). Used by kind permission of Shash Trevett; 'Fair Weather' from *The Complete Poems of Dorothy Parker* by Dorothy Parker, copyright © 1999 by The National Association for the Advancement of Colored People. Used by permission of Penguin Books, an imprint of Penguin Publishing Group, a division of Penguin Random House LLC. All rights reserved; 'Deep in the Hills' by Ruth Dallas, *Collected Poems*. Dunedin, Otago University Press, 2000; 'Angola' by Amélia Veiga, translated by Julia Kirst in *The Heinemann Book of African Women's Poetry*; 'O Earth' by Siriman Cissoko, *French African Verse* translated by Clive Wake and John O Reed, Heinemann; 'The Sash Window' by Rosemary Tonks from *Bedouin of the London Evening: Collected Poems* (Bloodaxe Books, 2014); 'The Echoes' by Mazisi Kunene by kind permission of the Mazisi Kunene Foundation Trust; 'Londoners' by Kristina Rungano 1984 in *A Storm is Brewing*, Zimbabwe Publishing House; 'An Old Colonial Building' originally appeared in *City at the End of Time: Poems* by Leung Ping-Kwan, pp. 87. Copyright © 2012 Reprinted by permission of Hong Kong University Press; 'Perhaps the World Ends Here', from *The Woman Who Fell from The Sky* by Joy Harjo. Copyright © 1994 by Joy Harjo. Used by permission of W W Norton & Company, Inc and of The Wylie Agency (UK) Limited; 'My Aunts Don't Want to Move' by Moniza Alvi from *Split World: Poems 1990–2005* (Bloodaxe Books, 2008); 'Map Store' by Iman Mersal translated by Robyn Creswell in *The Threshold: Poems* (Farrar, Straus & Giroux); 'Under These Stones' by Delores Gauntlett (nee McAnuff), 2007 *New Caribbean Poetry*, Carcanet, Edited by Kei Miller; 'Nomad in the Sunset' by Roza Mukasheva, translated by Hamid Ismailov, published in *The World Record (International Voices from Southbank Centre's Poetry Parnassus)* Bloodaxe Books, 2012, used by kind permission of Hamid Ismailov; 'Leaving Fingerprints' by Imtiaz Dharker from *Leaving Fingerprints* (Bloodaxe Books, 2009); 'The Ruin' by Jacob Polley from *The Havocs* (Picador, 2012) by kind permission of the author; 'Till' by Gregor Addison, used by permission of the author; 'I Pick Up My Footprints' by Vasyl Holoborodko, translated from the Ukranian by Svetlana Lavochkina, from *Words for War: New Poems from Ukraine* Copyright © 2017 by Borderlines Foundation for Academic Studies. Copyright © 2017 by Academic Studies Press. Reprinted with the permission of The Permissions Company, LLC on behalf of the publisher, academicstudiespress.com. All rights reserved; 'Sentinel' by Jennifer Anne Champion in *Caterwaul* Math Paper Press, 2016, used by permission of the author; 'Grandmothers Abroad' by Tishani Doshi from *A God at the Door* (Bloodaxe Books, 2021); 'Paradise' by Roger Robinson, *A Portable Paradise*, Peepal

Tree Press, 2019; 'Knots' by Jo Clement from *Outlandish* (Bloodaxe Books, 2022); 'Touchstone' by Olive Senior (*Hurricane Watch: New and Collected Poems*, 2022) is reprinted by permission of Carcanet Press, UK; 'Untitled' by Osip Mandelstam, translated by James Greene, 1989, in *Selected Poems* (Penguin), thanks to Angel Books; 'when faces called flowers float out of the ground' Copyright 1950, ©1978, 1991 by the Trustees for the E E Cummings Trust. Copyright ©1979 by George James Firmage, from *Complete Poems: 1904–1962* by E E Cummings, edited by George J. Firmage. Used by permission of Liveright Publishing Corporation; 'Song' by Seán Ó Ríordáin, translated by Ciarán Carson, used by permission of Cló Iar-Chonnacht; 'In Georgia' from Yevtushenko: *Selected Poems* by Yevgeny Yevtushenko published by Penguin Classics. Copyright © Yevgeny Yevtushenko, 1962. Reprinted by permission of Penguin Books Limited; 'The Day Lady Died' by Frank O'Hara from *Lunch Poems*. Copyright © 1964 by Frank O'Hara. Reprinted with the permission of The Permissions Company, LLC on behalf of City Lights Books, www.citylights.com; 'Allegro' from *The Half-Finished Heaven* by Tomas Tranströmer. Copyright © 2001 by Tomas Tranströmer. Translation copyright © 2001 by Robert Bly. Reprinted with the permission of The Permissions Company, LLC on behalf of Graywolf Press, graywolfpress.org and of Penguin Books Limited; 'The Joy of Writing' from *View with A Grain of Sand* by Wislawa Szymborska, translated by Stanislaw Baranczak and Clare Cavanagh. English Translation copyright © 1995 by HarperCollins Publishers. Used by permission of HarperCollins Publishers; 'Untitled' by Mario Luzi translated by Luigi Bonaffini in *For the Baptism of our Fragments* pub by Guernica Editions (Montreal),1992, used with permission of Luigi Bonaffini; 'Swimming After Thoughts' by Jay Parini, 1990 in *New and Collected Poems 1975–2015* by Beacon Press; 'Bouncing Boy' by Helen Dunmore from *Counting Backwards: Poems 1975–2017* (Bloodaxe Books, 2019); 'Captain of the Lighthouse' and 'Arguments Left' by Togara Muzanenhamo (*Spirit Brides*, 2006) are reprinted by permission of Carcanet Press, UK; 'Lightness' by Yvonne Gray, 2007 in *A New Orkney Anthology* GMB Writing Fellowship, used with permission of the author; 'Pier' by Vona Groarke from *Selected Poems* (2016) is reproduced by kind permission of the author and The Gallery Press, Loughcrew, Oldcastle, County Meath, Ireland. www.gallerypress.com; 'Common/wealth' by Nii Awikyei Parkes, 2012 in *Out of Bounds* by Bloodaxe Books used by permission of David Godwin Associates; 'Prologue (Grime Mix)' by Patience Agbabi from *Telling Tales*, Canongate Books, PLS Clear; 'Handfast' by Anthony Vahni Capildeo (*Measures of Expatriation*, 2016) is reprinted by permission of Carcanet Press, UK; 'Girl in the Blue Pool' by Helen Dunmore from *Counting Backwards: Poems 1975–2017* (Bloodaxe Books, 2019); 'The Kite' by Andrew Wynn Owen (*The Multiverse*, 2018) is reprinted by permission of Carcanet Press, UK; 'Huia' by Bill Manhire (*Wow*, 2020) is reprinted by permission of Carcanet Press, UK; 'Sea: NightSurfing in

Bolinas' by Forrest Gander, from *Twice Alive*, copyright © 2019, 2020, 2021 by Forrest Gander. Reprinted by permission of New Directions Publishing Corp; 'How to perfect a flip turn' by Cynthia Miller 2021 in *Honorifics* by Nine Arches Press; 'Lover's Return' by Langston Hughes from *The Collected Poems of Langston Hughes*, published by Alfred A Knopf Inc © The Estate of Langston Hughes, reproduced by permission of David Higham Associates Limited; 'The Poet Speaks to his Love on the Telephone' by Federico García Lorca, 1935 in *Selected Poems*, by Oxford World Classics, translated by Martin Sorrell, permission conveyed through Copyright Clearance Center, Inc; 'Sea Canes' by Derek Walcott in *Sea Grapes*, Faber and Faber; 'The Poppy Signals Time to Scythe the Wheat' by Mimi Khalvati (*Collected Poems*, 2024) is reprinted by permission of Carcanet Press, UK; 'Temporary Sanity' by Dambudzo Marechere in *Cemetery of Mind* by Baobab Books © The Dambudzo Marechera Trust; 'Transit' by Michael O'Siadhail from *Collected Poems* (Bloodaxe Books, 2013); 'Words Between Us' by Debjani Chaterjee from *A Little Bridge* by Debjani Chatterjee, Simon Fletcher and Basir Sultan Kazmi, with thanks to Pennine Pens; 'Song', Jennifer Rahim, *Between the Fence and the Forest*, Peepal Tree Press, 2007; 'The Sculpture' by Aminur Rahman, translated by Sundeep Sen, in *A Life Wrapped in Ease*, Morgan's Eye Press; 'A Feather' by Shakila Azzizzada, translated from Dari by Zuzanna Olszewska with the poet Mimi Khalvati. First published in *Poems* by The Poetry Translation Centre, 2012;

'Poet, Lover, Birdwatcher' by Nissim Ezekiel, reproduced with permission of Oxford University Press India © 1989; 'Arguments Left' by Togara Muzanenhamo (*Spirit Brides*, 2006) reprinted by permission of Carcanet Press, UK; 'In the Chill' by Sophie Hannah (*Marrying the Ugly Millionaire: New and Collected Poems*, 2015) is reprinted by permission of Carcanet Press, UK; 'Gloves' by Joanna Preston from *The Summer King*, (Otago University Press, 2009), by permission of the author; 'Fast Forward' by Fleur Adcock from *Collected Poems* (Bloodaxe Books, 2024); 'You May Have Heard of Me' by Shazea Quraishi from *The Art of Scratching* (Bloodaxe Books, 2015); 'Beloved' by Asha Lul Mohamud Yusuf, translated from Somali by Said Jama Hussein and Maxamed Xasan 'Alto' with the poet Clare Pollard. First published in *The Sea-Migrations* by The Poetry Translation Centre and Bloodaxe Books, 2017; 'Ode to a Pot Noodle' from *Antiemetic for Homesickness* by Romalyn Ante published by Chatto & Windus. Copyright © Romalyn Ante, 2020. Reprinted by permission of The Random House Group Limited; 'Netezon Laundrette' by Charlotte Van Den Broek from *The Inside of a Stone*, translated by David Colmer (Bloodaxe Books, 2025); 'Dedication' from *Selected Poetry* by Johanne Wolfgang von Goethe, translated by David Luke and published by Penguin Classics. Copyright © David Luke, 1999. Reprinted by permission of Penguin Books Limited; 'What the Heart is Like' by Miroslav Holub from *Poems Before & After: Collected English Translations*, translated by Ian & Jarmila Milner et al. (Bloodaxe

Books, 2006); 'The Widower in the Country' by Les Murray (*New Collected Poems*, 2003) is reprinted by permission of Carcanet Press, UK; 'Solitude' from *The Half-Finished Heaven: The Best Poems of Tomas Tranströmer* Copyright © 2001 by Tomas Tranströmer. Translation copyright © 2001 by Robert Bly. Reprinted with the permission of The Permissions Company, LLC on behalf of Graywolf Press, graywolfpress.org and Penguin Classics. Copyright © Tomas Tranströmer, 2018. Reprinted by permission of Penguin Books Limited; Two poems from *Letters to Martha and Other Poems from a South African Prison* by Dennis Brutus, Heinemann; 'Epitaph' by Tchicaya U Tam'si, translated by Gerald Moore in *Selected Poems*, Heinemann; 'You Won't Believe It', by Simin Behbahani, translated from the Persian by Kaveh Safa and Farzaneh Milani in *A Cup of Sin: Selected Poems* (Syracuse University Press © 1999). Reproduced with permission from the publisher; 'Mistress of My Own Being' by Ifi Amadiume, by kind permission of the author; 'What I Learned in the Wars' by Yehuda Amichai, translated by Karen Alkalay-Gut, in *The American Voice Anthology of Poetry* by University Press of Kentucky; 'Narcissus at the Flea Market' by John Agard from *Travel Light, Travel Dark* (Bloodaxe Books, 2013); 'Bones' by Arundathi Subramaniam from *When God is a Traveller* (Bloodaxe Books, 2014); 'The Way I Am' from *Introducing George The Poet* by George The Poet published by Virgin Books. Copyright © George Mpanga, 2015. Reprinted by permission of The Random House Group Limited; 'Kindness' by Naomi Shihab Nye from *Tender Spot: Selected Poems* (Bloodaxe Books; BOA, 2015) and Far Corner Books; '*Kumukanda*' by Kayo Chingonyi published by Chatto & Windus. Copyright © Kayo Chingonyi, 2017. Reprinted by permission of The Random House Group Limited; 'Maracas Beach Prayer' by Roger Robinson, *A Portable Paradise*, Peepal Tree Press, 2019; 'The Day' by © Mukahang Limbu, 2021. Published in *Oxford Poetry* (2021) and *The Forward Book of Poetry 2023* (Forward Arts Foundation in association with Faber & Faber, 2023); 'Picture of Girl and a Small Boy (Burji, Gaza, 2017)' by Marjorie Lotfi from *The Wrong Person to Ask* (Bloodaxe Books, 2023)

Cover Mongkol Chuewong/Getty Images